DEPARTMENT OF TRUTH
UNITED STATES OF AMERICA
DEPARTMENT OF
GUANTANAMO BAY
CITF-G/SAC
legal proceedings.

THE DEPARTMENT OF TRUTH

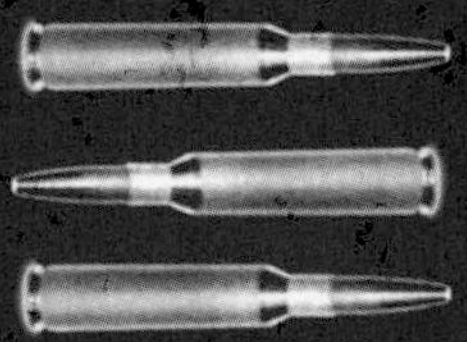

VOLUME 01:

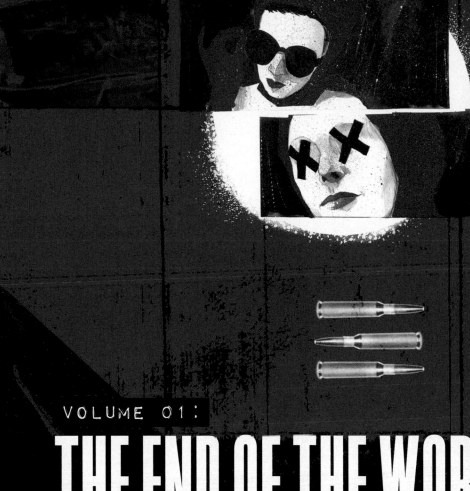

THE END OF THE WORLD

WRITER: >>>>>>
JAMES TYNION IV

ARTIST: >>>>>>
MARTIN SIMMONDS

LETTERER: >>>>>>
ADITYA BIDIKAR

DESIGNER: >>>>>>
DYLAN TODD

EDITOR: >>>>>>
STEVE FOXE

DEPARTMENT OF TRUTH ★ UNITED STATES OF AMERICA ★

THE DEPARTMENT OF TRUTH, VOL. 1. First printing. February 2021. Published by Image Comics, Inc. Office of publication: PO BOX 14457, Portland, OR 97293. Printed in the USA. For international rights, contact: foreignlicensing@imagecomics.com.

Standard ISBN: 978-1-5343-1833-5.
Forbidden Planet Exclusive ISBN: 978-1-5343-1970-7.
Indigo Exclusive ISBN: 978-1-5343-1978-3.
Newbury Comics Exclusive ISBN: 978-1-5343-1971-4.
OASAS Exclusive ISBN: 978-1-5343-1973-8.
Sanctum Sanctorum Exclusive ISBN: 978-1-5343-1972-1.
Third Eye Exclusive ISBN: 978-1-5343-1974-5.
Variant Edition Exclusive ISBN: 978-1-5343-1969-1.

TINY ONION TINYONIONSTUDIOS.COM

image

DALLAS, TX.
November 22, 1963.
7:55 p.m.
I'D LIKE SOME LEGAL REPRESENTATION. THESE POLICE OFFICERS HAVE NOT ALLOWED ME TO HAVE ANY...
I DON'T KNOW WHAT THIS IS ALL ABOUT.
DID YOU SHOOT THE PRESIDENT?
I WORK IN THAT BUILDING.
WERE YOU IN THE BUILDING AT THAT TIME?
NATURALLY, IF I WORK IN THAT BUILDING. YES, SIR.
DID YOU SHOOT THE PRESIDENT?
THEY'RE TAKING ME IN BECAUSE OF THE FACT THAT I LIVED IN THE SOVIET UNION.
I'M JUST A PATSY!
DID YOU SHOOT THE PRESIDENT?!

WE'RE GOING TO NEED THE ROOM.
THAT WASN'T A REQUEST.
HIT ME IN THE--
LEE.
I'M NOT... I'M NOT THE PERSON THEY ALL THINK I AM! I'M NOT THIS--
LEE. NOBODY IS LISTENING.
IT'S JUST US IN THIS ROOM.
...
I DIDN'T THINK IT WOULD REALLY HAPPEN.
NONE OF THAT MATTERS ANYMORE.

WHAT DO THEY BELIEVE JUST HAPPENED? WHAT DO THE PEOPLE THINK--
THAT'S WHAT WE'RE HERE TO SETTLE.
SOMETHING THIS BIG. THIS MOMENT IS GOING TO HAVE CONSEQUENCES. THINGS ARE GOING TO CHANGE.
THIS WORLD IS GOING TO CHANGE.
CAN'T FUCKING REMEMBER WHAT REALLY HAPPENED... IS THAT... IS IT HAPPENING TO ME? I'M A PART OF IT NOW, AREN'T I?
YES.
I WAS SENT HERE TO TELL YOU WHAT'S GOING TO HAPPEN NEXT.
AND THEN WE'RE GOING TO TRY AND MAKE SURE EVERYBODY ELSE UNDERSTANDS THAT, TOO. DO YOU FOLLOW?
YES.
SHIT. YES. I UNDERSTAND.
GOOD. NOW SAY IT. SAY IT SO I KNOW YOU STILL REMEMBER.
SAY IT SO I KNOW YOU KNOW THE TRUTH.
UP IS DOWN AND DOWN IS UP.

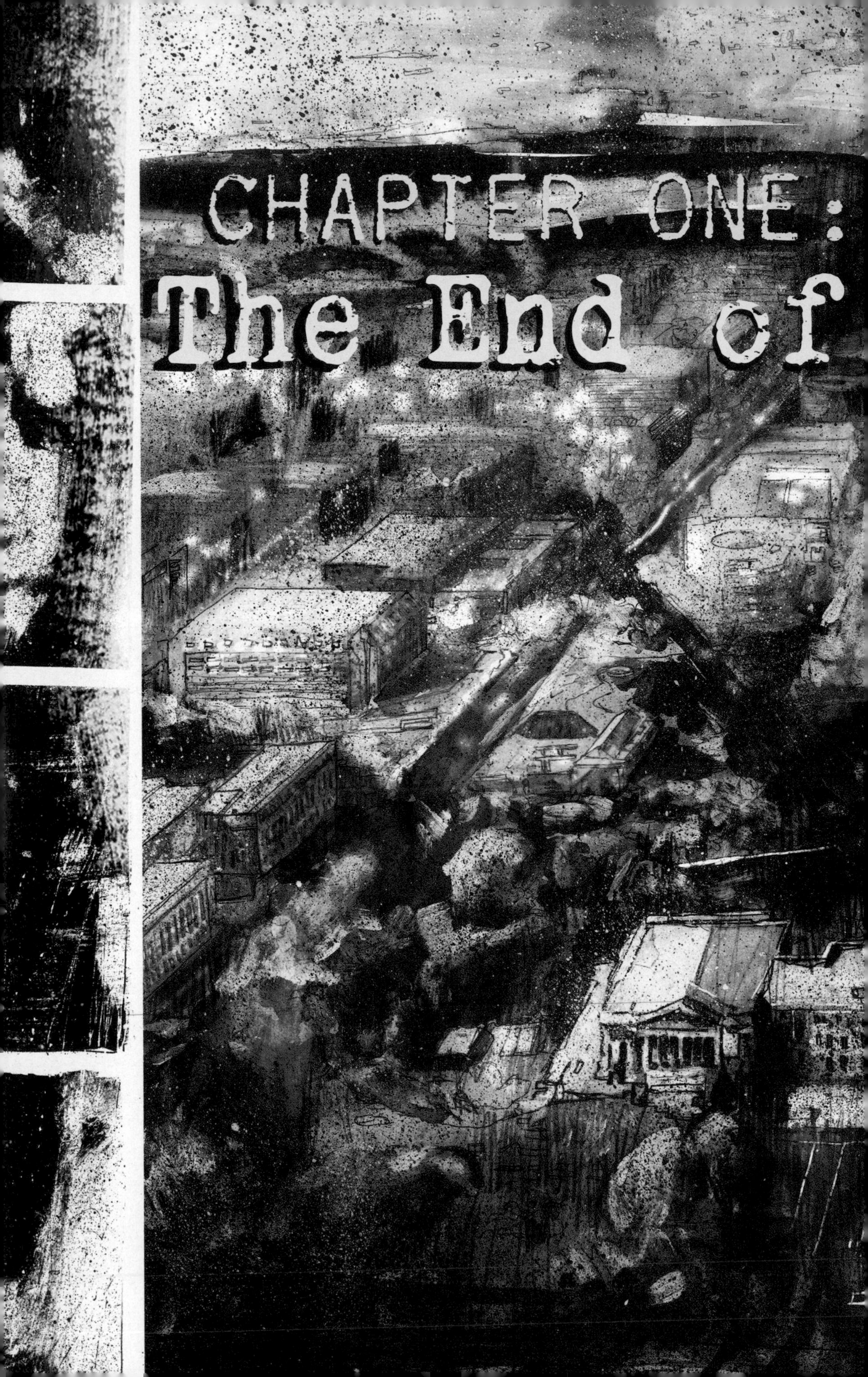

CHAPTER ONE:
The End of

the World

YOU GOING TO THROW UP?
NO.
MAYBE.
DON'T THROW UP.
OKAY.
ARE YOU GOING TO KILL ME, TOO?
JUST DON'T THROW UP. THE LAST CAR THEY GAVE ME WAS SHIT. I LIKE THIS CAR.
OKAY.

THE LIBRARY OF CONGRESS.
Present Day.
ARE YOU--?
DID YOU SEE IT, TOO? DID YOU SEE IT, OR AM I JUST COMPLETELY LOSING MY MIND?
YEAH, OKAY. YOU'RE GOING TO KILL ME.
IF YOU KEEP ASKING QUESTIONS, YEAH. PROBABLY.

TELL ME YOUR NAME, KID.
COLE. I'M COLE.
DO YOU KNOW WHY YOU'RE HERE?
I'M HERE... BECAUSE I SAW SOME-THING. SOMETHING THAT CAN'T POSSIBLY EXIST. AND NOW I THINK YOU'RE GOING TO KILL ME.
HAH.
HE'S FUNNY.
HE'S NOT JOKING.
I KNOW. I DIDN'T MEAN HE WAS ACTUALLY FUNNY.

FBI.
YES, SIR.
QUANTICO. YOU'RE A TEACHER.
I...I'VE DONE SOME FIELD WORK.
BUT YOU'RE A TEACHER. YOU TEACH ABOUT FUNNY PICTURES ON THE INTERNET.
I, *UH*...I LOOK INTO THE SORTS OF DISCUSSIONS THAT HAPPEN AMONG RIGHT-WING WHITE NATIONALISTS IN THEIR ONLINE COMMUNITIES.
FUNNY PICTURES. THEY SHARE FUNNY PICTURES.
THEY AREN'T FUNNY. THEY'RE TYPICALLY NOT THAT ORIGINAL, AND... WELL. THEY'RE VERY RACIST.
THEY THINK THEY'RE FUNNY, I MEAN.
YEAH. I GUESS... YEAH.

AND THEN THERE'S THE CONSPIRACY THEORY STUFF.
UH... WELL, YES.
TELL ME ABOUT THAT.
I...I DON'T KNOW...
SON. YOU'RE JUST GOING TO HAVE TO GET OVER WHETHER OR NOT WE'RE GOING TO KILL YOU. I JUST WANT YOU TO FUCKING TALK TO US.
WHAT DO YOUR LITTLE MESSAGE BOARDS HAVE TO DO WITH CONSPIRACY THEORIES?
THEIR ERR...PERSPECTIVE ON THE WORLD. THEIR BELIEF THAT THE SYSTEM IS STACKED AGAINST THEM IN DELIBERATE WAYS. IT MAKES THEM... WELL, SUSCEPTIBLE TO INFLUENCE.
THAT'S WHAT I'VE BEEN STUDYING. THEIR... SUSCEPTIBILITY.

AND THAT'S HOW YOU GOT TO THE FLAT EARTH CONFERENCE.
YES.
START AT THE BEGINNING.
SIR, I WAS DRINKING OVER THE WEEKEND. AND I HAVEN'T SLEPT-- REALLY SLEPT-- IN ABOUT THREE DAYS.
NONE OF THIS...THE SORT OF THINGS I THINK I SAW...
I DO NOT TRUST MY MEMORIES, AND I DON'T SEE ANY REASON YOU SHOULD EITHER.
GOOD. THAT'S A VERY SENSIBLE ATTITUDE.
NOW TELL ME WHAT YOU SAW.

I remember walking into the hotel conference area and thinking that I had never seen so many polo shirts in my life.
Your mailman. Your accountant. The guy who scans your plane ticket at the airport. They were mostly, but not exclusively, men. Mostly, but not exclusively, white.
Just ordinary, boring people. Making jokes about the latest episode of a network TV show, or quoting an old *Family Guy*.
That's what struck me the most. You'd never pick them out in a crowd. They were anybody and everybody and nobody.
And they all had this grin on their face. A grin that said they knew a secret truth about this world. Something nobody else knew.
They believed the earth was flat.
That all scientific research to the contrary is a conspiracy to make us docile, so the government can feed us the facts they want us believe.
THE FLAT EARTH SOCIETY
ANNUAL GATHERING

Well, some believe it's the government, some believe it's the church, and some have more...colorful suggestions.
FLAT EARTH AND THE PROTOCOLS OF THE ELDERS OF ZION
They buy maps and models of the world for their homes and offices, to hang up next to their signed comic books and movie posters.
They listen to self-taught basement physicists twist scientific theory to their cause.
And then they drink at the hotel bar, and have the sort of excited arguments where they egg each other on, convinced they're going to get closer to the truth tomorrow.

WHY DO YOU THINK THEY BELIEVE?
IT'S...IT'S ALWAYS ABOUT CONTROL. THAT'S WHAT I THINK.
IT'S A DESIRE TO REJECT THE ASPECTS OF LIFE THAT FEEL TOO COMPLICATED AND TOO ABSTRACT, AND BUILD A MORE COMFORTABLE REALITY THAT THEY CAN UNDERSTAND.
AND MORE THAN THAT...IT'S A SENSE...THAT IF THEY'RE RIGHT, AND THEY'RE ONTO THE TRUTH THAT'S BEEN KEPT SECRET ALL THIS TIME...
WELL, THEN THEY'RE HEROES, AREN'T THEY?
STANDING UP AGAINST THE AUTHORITY THAT'S TRYING TO KEEP THEM AND THEIR FRIENDS AND FAMILY DOWN.
THEY WANT REALITY TO MAKE SENSE IN A WAY THAT MAKES THEM IMPORTANT, AND SPECIAL.
EVERYONE WANTS TO FEEL LIKE THAT, RIGHT?
HEH.
WHAT?
TELL ME WHEN IT WENT SIDEWAYS.

YOU'RE COLE TURNER.
I, UH... YES.
SPECIAL AGENT COLE TURNER.
YES.
WHY DON'T YOU COME WITH ME?
I... I DON'T THINK... I SHOULD?
I HAVE... I'M MARRIED. I HAVE A HUSBAND AT HOME... I'M JUST... GOING TO BED?
YOU SHOULD COME WITH ME.
THIS IS ONE OF THOSE MOMENTS. THE MOMENTS THAT CHANGE YOUR LIFE. THE MOMENTS THAT CHANGE EVERY-THING?
DON'T YOU WANT THAT?
-GULP-

AH, MR. TURNER.
HE CAME. MARVELOUS, HE CAME. THANK YOU, SEBASTIAN.
OF COURSE. I'LL LEAVE YOU TO IT.
NICE MEETING YOU.
UH, YEAH.
YOU KNOW WHO WE ARE?
KENNETH AND BERTRAM BOULET.
I LOVE WHEN THEY KNOW WHO WE ARE. DON'T YOU, BERTIE?
YOU WERE AT OUR LITTLE CARNIVAL TODAY, WEREN'T YOU? WALKING AROUND WITH THE LITTLE PEOPLE.
YES, SIR.
KEN. PLEASE.
IT'S MARVELOUS. THERE'S MORE EACH YEAR. THAT'S WHAT MAKES THIS ALL POSSIBLE.

THAT AND PEOPLE LIKE YOU.
LIKE ME?
WE HAVE MANY FRIENDS IN WASHINGTON, YOUNG MAN. EVEN IF THEY DON'T SEE EYE TO EYE, THEY HELP US MAKE ALL THIS POSSIBLE. IF WE KEEP THE WHEELS GREASED.
BUT WE'VE BEEN WANTING TO RECRUIT A BELIEVER. SOMEONE IN INTELLIGENCE. AND THEN YOU STUMBLED INTO OUR LITTLE PARTY.
NOW, SON, DO YOU **BELIEVE?**
I remember how terrible his breath was. That's what stuck in my mind.
The fortune from their Texas Oil company had been funding right-wing politicians for the last two decades.
I remember thinking, how does a man worth billions of dollars have such terrible breath?
But that's not what I said. What I said was...
YES. I BELIEVE.

They took me into a little side room. Not much bigger than this. There were other people there. All men. All white. All dressed in suits...Except...
There was a woman, dressed in red. She was wearing these sunglasses in the dark room, and it scared me. I don't know why it scared me so much...
I just knew she couldn't see wearing those things, and I got this pit in my stomach.
It got worse when she SMILED at me.
There was a film playing, in black and white, on an old projector.
As it played, the men in the room leaned in. There was this smell in the air. This...I don't know. It was like a smug musk.
Anticipation on the edge of orgasm.
Like we were watching something obscene and decadent.
It was the moon rover. The landing. The shot of Neil Armstrong descending the ladder, ready to make his one small step for man.
But there was something off about it. I couldn't put my finger on it at first, but I quickly realized.

The angle of the shot was all wrong. It was from a different vantage point. I was trying to figure out why when I saw something in the dark behind the lunar rover.
It was a man, holding a cardboard cup of coffee. No space helmet, no anything. Just this ordinary, tired-looking man on the moon.
The room erupted as they saw him. But I just broke out in a nervous sweat.
The Boulets said it was from Kubrick's private collection. That it'd been held in a government warehouse for the last few decades.
They talked about a plan to release it to the press, in due time. But that it would need to be coordinated with their BIGGER find.
That's when one of the brothers leaned in and asked me if I wanted to take a trip with them, and see how deep the rabbit hole went.

WHY DID YOU GO?
THE BOULETS FUND MOST OF THE CORNERS OF THE INTERNET I STUDY. THE EXTREMIST CORNERS. HONESTLY, I THOUGHT I WAS COMING IN AT THE GROUND FLOOR OF SOMETHING.
THEM TRYING TO CREATE THEIR OWN CONSPIRACY THEORY TO FEED THE TROLLS AND KEEP THEM AGITATED AND PLIABLE.
THAT'S NOT WHY. YOU WANTED TO SEE SOMETHING THAT WOULD MAKE SENSE OF ALL OF THIS BULLSHIT. BECAUSE IT DIDN'T FEEL LIKE IT HAD BEEN DOCTORED...
AND IF THAT VIDEO WASN'T BULLSHIT, IT MEANT A WHOLE LOT ELSE YOU BELIEVE **IS** BULLSHIT.
OKAY, YEAH. THAT'S WHY.
AND I'D NEVER BEEN ON A PRIVATE PLANE BEFORE.
THEY SAID THEIR GOVERNMENT CONTACTS WERE COVERING FOR ME. BUT THEY WOULDN'T TELL ME WHERE THEY WERE GOING. THEY DIDN'T WANT TO SPOIL THE SURPRISE.
THE OTHER MEN, THEY DRANK THE WHOLE TIME. I MIGHT HAVE HAD A GLASS OR TWO, BUT MOSTLY I STARED OUT THE WINDOW...
YOU WANTED TO SEE THE CURVATURE OF THE EARTH, WITH YOUR OWN EYES. AND I'M SURE YOU DID, BUT THERE WAS THIS SENSE THAT MAYBE IT WAS JUST YOUR IMAGINATION.
YOU DIDN'T TRUST WHAT YOU WERE SEEING, DID YOU?
NO.
I DIDN'T.

I don't know how long the flight was...
It felt like days. And I don't know. It may have been. We stopped to refuel a few times.
I can't imagine what my husband was thinking.
The party was continuing, and you could just feel the stench of excitement in the air. The plane felt thick with it.
And I just sat, feeling sick in my seat. Time melted away. I felt... unmoored more than anything. Hungover from what I'd seen in that screening room.
I had dozed off, when a hand shook my shoulder.
COLE. YOU'RE MISSING IT. YOU'RE AT THE END OF EVERYTHING, AND YOU'RE MISSING THE DAMN SHOW.
LOOK OUT YOUR WINDOW, AND SEE WHAT THEY'VE BEEN HIDING FROM US, ALL THESE YEARS.
WHAT... WHERE ARE WE...?
WE'RE OFF THE EDGE OF THE MAP, BOY.
HERE THERE BE MONSTERS.

OH. OH, JESUS.
YES, PRAISE JESUS.
I NEED... I NEED TO...
MOVE. I NEED THE BATHROOM... I NEED.
DID YOU SEE?
IT'S IMPORTANT THAT YOU SEE..
FUCKING HELL...

ALRIGHT, GENTS. WE'LL BE LANDING AT THE BASECAMP IN A MOMENT. FROM THERE WE CAN TAKE A HELICOPTER UP CLOSE.
WE STILL HAVEN'T FOUND THE TOP OF THE THING. WHERE IT MEETS THE SKY...BUT WE'LL TAKE YOU AS HIGH AS WE CAN GO.
SEATBELTS. THIS IS GOING TO BE BUMPY.
HK HUURK

I'M SORRY, DEAR, BUT DO YOU WORK FOR US?
DOES SHE LOOK LIKE SHE WORKS FOR US, BERTIE?
WHO SENT YOU? ARE YOU FROM BLACK HAT?
NOPE.

COLE TURNER?
SPECIAL AGENT COLE TURNER?
Y-YES.
YES.
I'M HERE TO TAKE YOU HOME.

THAT'S ALL I KNOW. YOU CAN KILL ME NOW.
WE'RE NOT GOING TO FUCKING KILL YOU. CALM DOWN.
WHAT DO YOU THINK, RUBY?
HE'S FINE.
YEAH?
YEAH. HE'LL DO. HE'S IN SHOCK, BUT HE KEPT ALL THE IMPORTANT DETAILS.
I COULD USE SOMEONE A BIT MORE PLUGGED IN TO THE MOMENT. NOT ANOTHER COLD WAR UFO HUNTER WITH A TINFOIL HAT.
AND YOU KNOW HIS HISTORY. WHAT HE WAS A PART OF IN THE '80S.
WHAT'S HAPPENING?
WE'RE **POACHING** YOU. YOU'VE BEEN POACHED. YOU DON'T WORK FOR THE FBI ANYMORE. YOU WORK FOR US.
I DON'T...I DON'T UNDERSTAND.

SON, THE WORLD IS ROUND.
IT GOES AROUND THE SUN. GET ME A BIG LASER POINTER AND A FEW METER STICKS AND I CAN PROVE IT TO YOU.
BUT THAT'S NOT THE TRUTH BECAUSE OF SCIENCE.
THAT'S THE **TRUTH.**
WHAT YOU SAW THERE, AT THE END OF THE WORLD, WAS A SLIVER OF ANOTHER KIND OF TRUTH TAKING HOLD.
YOU'RE SAYING IT WAS A KIND OF TULPA...SPACE?
WHEN THE FUCK DID THE WHOLE FUCKING WORLD GO BUDDHIST?
YOU'RE ALL GOING TO BE SHAVING YOUR HEAD AND SINGING TO ME WITH THIS HIPPY BULLSHIT...
THAT'S HARE KRISHNA.
I'M BEING FUNNY.
YOU'RE BEING HORRIBLE.
A TULPA IS A THOUGHTFORM... A BELIEF GIVEN A BODY.
I KNOW WHAT A FUCKING TULPA IS, COLE. JESUS. AND YOU'RE PART-RIGHT. YOU'RE JUST MISSING THE SCALE OF THE THING.
I'M GOING TO TELL YOU THE SECRET. THE BIG SECRET THAT YOU'VE KNOWN YOUR ENTIRE LIFE.

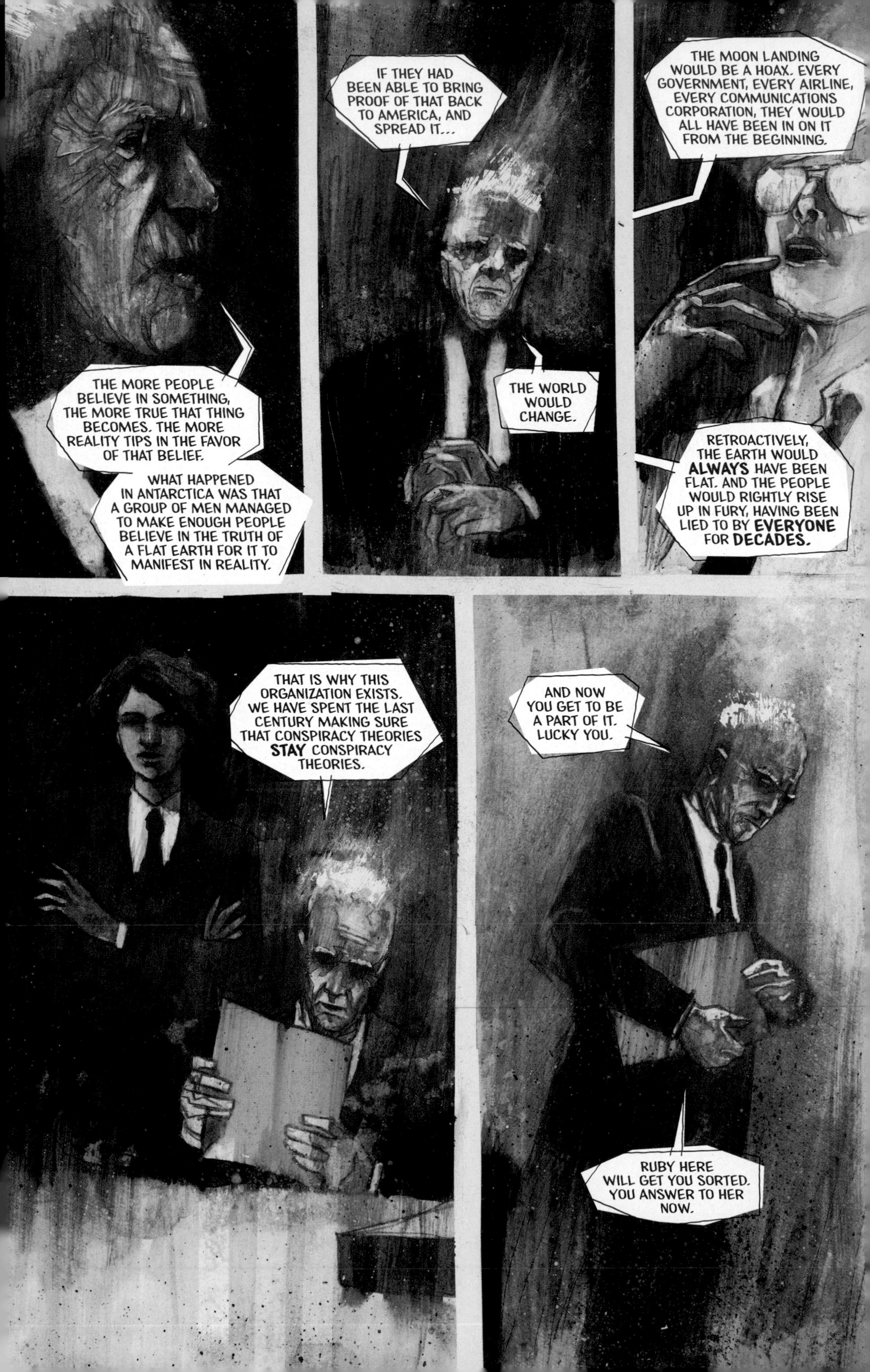
THE MORE PEOPLE BELIEVE IN SOMETHING, THE MORE TRUE THAT THING BECOMES. THE MORE REALITY TIPS IN THE FAVOR OF THAT BELIEF.
WHAT HAPPENED IN ANTARCTICA WAS THAT A GROUP OF MEN MANAGED TO MAKE ENOUGH PEOPLE BELIEVE IN THE TRUTH OF A FLAT EARTH FOR IT TO MANIFEST IN REALITY.
IF THEY HAD BEEN ABLE TO BRING PROOF OF THAT BACK TO AMERICA, AND SPREAD IT...
THE WORLD WOULD CHANGE.
THE MOON LANDING WOULD BE A HOAX. EVERY GOVERNMENT, EVERY AIRLINE, EVERY COMMUNICATIONS CORPORATION, THEY WOULD ALL HAVE BEEN IN ON IT FROM THE BEGINNING.
RETROACTIVELY, THE EARTH WOULD **ALWAYS** HAVE BEEN FLAT. AND THE PEOPLE WOULD RIGHTLY RISE UP IN FURY, HAVING BEEN LIED TO BY **EVERYONE** FOR **DECADES.**
THAT IS WHY THIS ORGANIZATION EXISTS. WE HAVE SPENT THE LAST CENTURY MAKING SURE THAT CONSPIRACY THEORIES **STAY** CONSPIRACY THEORIES.
AND NOW YOU GET TO BE A PART OF IT. LUCKY YOU.
RUBY HERE WILL GET YOU SORTED. YOU ANSWER TO HER NOW.

WAIT...I HAVE QUESTIONS.
I WOULDN'T WANT YOU IF YOU DIDN'T HAVE QUESTIONS. THERE WILL BE TIME FOR ALL THAT.
WHO WAS THE WOMAN IN RED WITH NO EYES? WHY DID THEY THINK RUBY WORKED FOR SOME-THING CALLED BLACK HAT?
SON, YOU KNOW DAMN WELL EACH OF THOSE QUESTIONS WILL LEAD TO MORE QUESTIONS, AND MORE QUESTIONS AFTER THAT.
AT LEAST WAIT UNTIL WE'RE PAYING YOU, FOR GOD'S SAKE.
LOOK, I STILL DON'T EVEN KNOW WHO THE HELL YOU PEOPLE ARE...
HEH, I GUESS I SKIPPED THAT PART, DIDN'T I?

DEPARTMENT OF TRUTH
UNITED ST
AMERICA
MY NAME IS LEE HARVEY OSWALD.
WELCOME TO THE DEPARTMENT OF TRUTH.

DEPARTMEN
UNITED STATES

CHAPTER 2

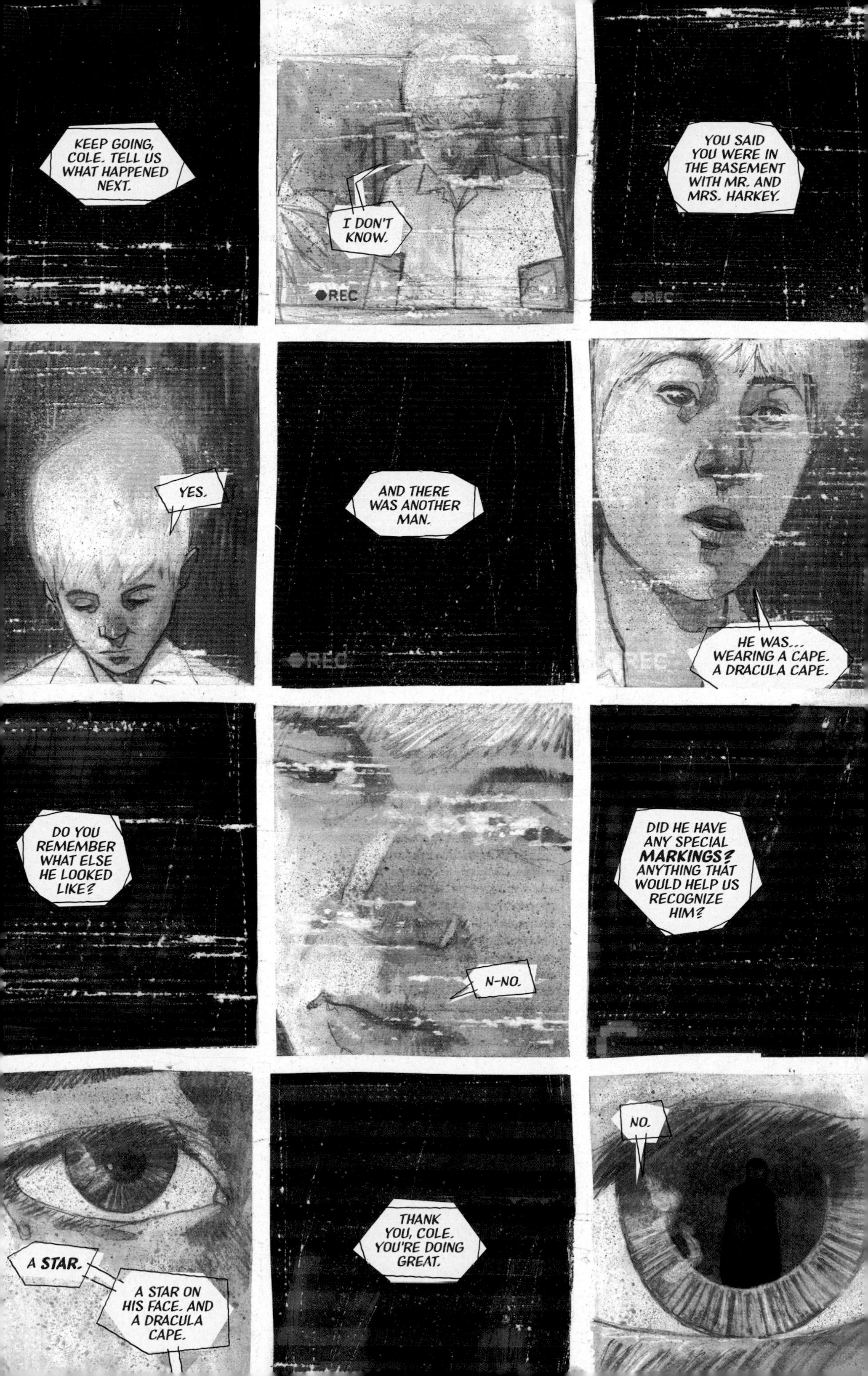
KEEP GOING, COLE. TELL US WHAT HAPPENED NEXT.
I DON'T KNOW.
●REC
YOU SAID YOU WERE IN THE BASEMENT WITH MR. AND MRS. HARKEY.
YES.
AND THERE WAS ANOTHER MAN.
●REC
HE WAS... WEARING A CAPE. A DRACULA CAPE.
DO YOU REMEMBER WHAT ELSE HE LOOKED LIKE?
N-NO.
DID HE HAVE ANY SPECIAL MARKINGS? ANYTHING THAT WOULD HELP US RECOGNIZE HIM?
A STAR.
A STAR ON HIS FACE. AND A DRACULA CAPE.
THANK YOU, COLE. YOU'RE DOING GREAT.
NO.

ARE YOU TIRED? WOULD YOU LIKE TO TAKE A BREAK?
THE STAR-FACED MAN, HE SAID...
IT'S OKAY, COLE. NONE OF THIS IS REAL.

THIS BABY ISN'T REAL. YOU CAN'T TASTE ITS MEAT. YOU CAN'T SMELL ITS BLOOD.
THIS IS ALL A DREAM LIKE YOUR MAMMA SAYS. LIKE YOUR TEACHER SAYS.
I'M A DREAM MAN, AND YOUR TEACHER LET ME IN.
AND I'M HUNNNNNGRY.
YOU DON'T HAVE TO WORRY. NONE OF THIS COUNTS.
IT'S NOT REAL SO IT DOESN'T COUNT.
YOU JUST CAN'T WAKE UP UNTIL I SAY SO.
OR HEEEEE'LL FIND YOU, AND GOOOOOOBBBLE YOU UP.
HE SAID NOT TO TALK.
IT'S OKAY, COLE, YOU CAN TALK TO ME.
HE SAID NO. HE SAID THE DEVIL KNOWS. HE SAID HE'D FIND ME.
I WANT TO WAKE UP. I WANT TO WAKE UP.
I WANT TO WAKE UP!
SIGH OKAY. STOP THE TAPE.

CHAPTER
TWO

YOU DIDN'T SLEEP.
I SLEPT.
YOU WERE STARING AT THE CEILING AT 5 A.M.
IT SOUNDS LIKE YOU DIDN'T SLEEP.
I NEVER SLEEP. I AM TERRIBLE AT SLEEPING. YOU NORMALLY SLEEP LIKE A ROCK.
I SLEPT FINE, MATTY.
OKAY.
DON'T DO THAT.
DO WHAT?
SAY OKAY LIKE THAT. LIKE IT'S GOING TO BE A FIGHT LATER.
I THINK I AM BEING VERY REASONABLE GIVEN THE FACT THAT MY HUSBAND DISAPPEARED FOR A FEW DAYS LAST WEEK AND WON'T TELL ME WHY.
OKAY.
YOU'VE LEARNED MY EVIL TRICKS.
MATTY...
WHAT'S UP?

LET'S SAY YOU COULD FIND OUT THAT ONE BIG CONSPIRACY THEORY WAS TRUE. LIKE YOU COULD PICK AND MAKE IT REAL AND FIND OUT ALL THE SECRETS BEHIND IT.
WHAT CRAZY CONSPIRACY THEORY DO YOU WANT ALL THE ANSWERS TO?
HMMM. I VOTE REPTILIANS.
REPTILIANS.
THE SHAPE-SHIFTING LIZARD ILLUMINATI THAT RULE OUR WORLD. THERE ARE VIDEOS ON YOUTUBE THAT SHOW DICK CHENEY BLINKING SIDEWAYS WITH VERTICAL EYE SLITS.
YOU KNOW? LIKE THE GUY AT THE START OF *MEN IN BLACK?*
WAIT. I SHOULD HAVE SAID THE MEN IN BLACK, SHOULDN'T I? ALIENS WOULD BE COOL.
NO. I WANT TO ASK LIZARD DICK CHENEY SOME HARD-HITTING QUESTIONS AND THEN TRY NOT TO GET LAUGHED OUT OF THE *POST* EDITORIAL MEETINGS WHEN I GO TO REPORT THEM.
I DIDN'T THINK THEY LET PROOFREADERS INTO THOSE MEETINGS.
THAT WAS BEFORE I GOT TAPPED BY THE REPTILIAN ILLUMINATI TO RUN THE PAPER.
AND YOU'RE GOING TO OUT THEM, AFTER THEY GOT YOU A CUSHY JOB?
FAIR POINT.
I KNOW WHAT **YOU'D** ASK ABOUT.
YEAH.
THIS ISN'T A FUN ASIDE, IS IT? WHAT'S WRONG?

I'M SORRY. MY JOB. IT'S... DRAGGING THINGS UP.
STARFACE.
YEAH.
HE'S NOT REAL. THOSE FUCKERS AND THEIR PUPPETS JUST LED YOU--
I KNOW.
HE'S ABOUT AS REAL AS THE REPTILIANS.
YEAH.
CAN YOU TALK ABOUT WHAT'S BOTHERING YOU?
NO. I'M SORRY. I REALLY CAN'T.
OKAY, THEN. YOU KNOW I LOVE YOU?
YES.

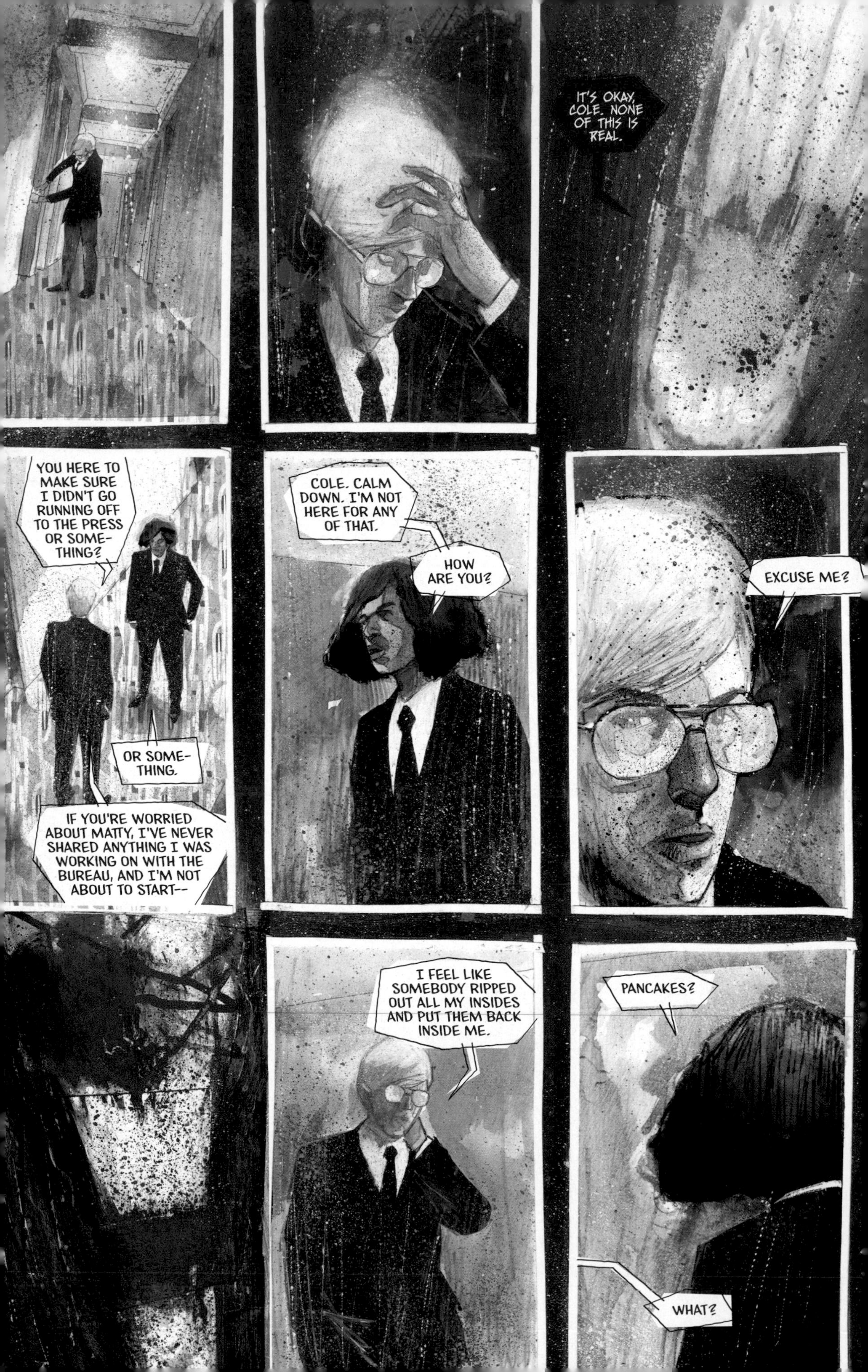
IT'S OKAY, COLE. NONE OF THIS IS REAL.
YOU HERE TO MAKE SURE I DIDN'T GO RUNNING OFF TO THE PRESS OR SOME-THING?
OR SOME-THING.
IF YOU'RE WORRIED ABOUT MATTY, I'VE NEVER SHARED ANYTHING I WAS WORKING ON WITH THE BUREAU, AND I'M NOT ABOUT TO START--
COLE. CALM DOWN. I'M NOT HERE FOR ANY OF THAT.
HOW ARE YOU?
EXCUSE ME?
I FEEL LIKE SOMEBODY RIPPED OUT ALL MY INSIDES AND PUT THEM BACK INSIDE ME.
PANCAKES?
WHAT?

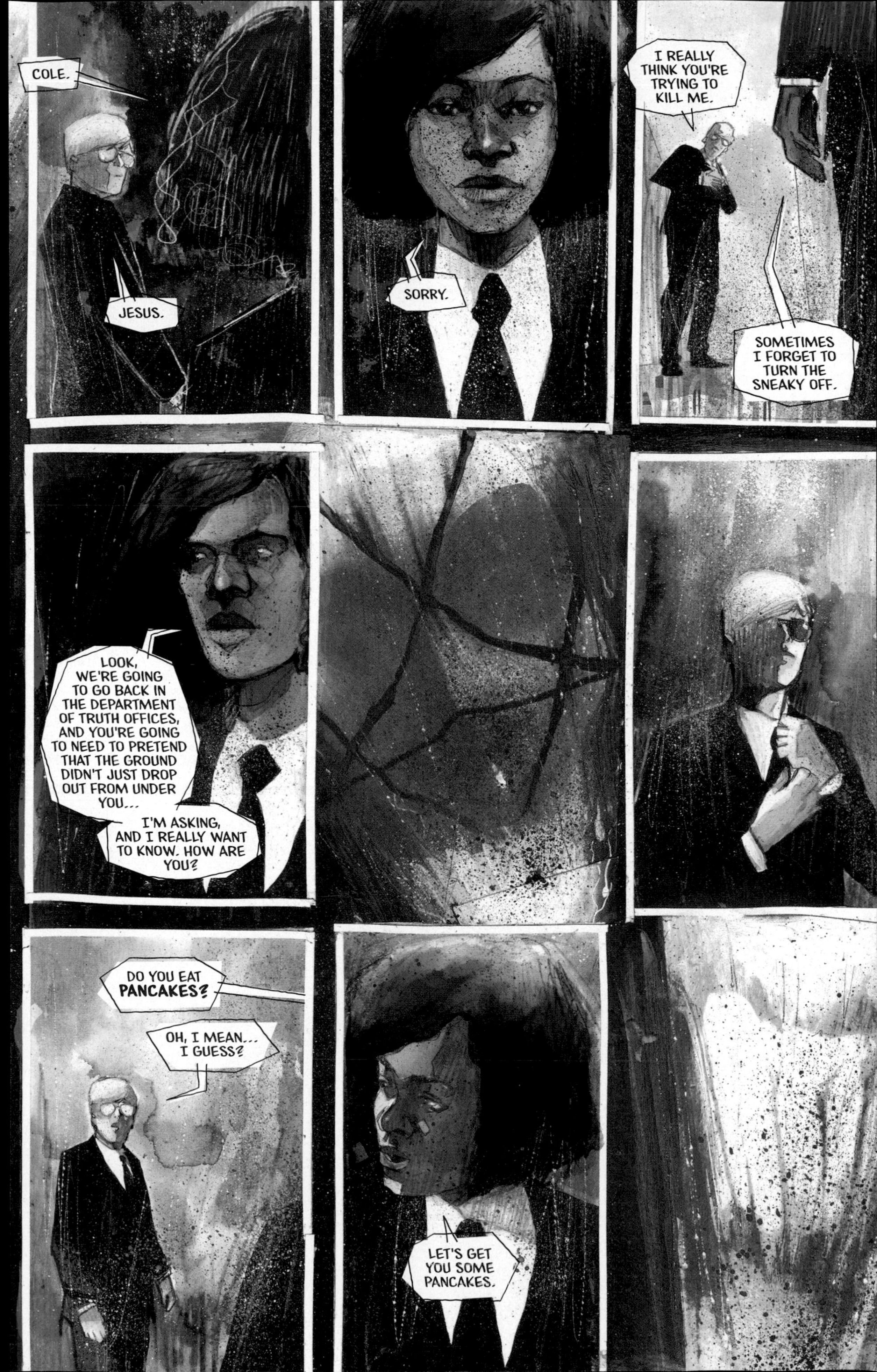
COLE.
JESUS.
SORRY.
I REALLY THINK YOU'RE TRYING TO KILL ME.
SOMETIMES I FORGET TO TURN THE SNEAKY OFF.
LOOK, WE'RE GOING TO GO BACK IN THE DEPARTMENT OF TRUTH OFFICES, AND YOU'RE GOING TO NEED TO PRETEND THAT THE GROUND DIDN'T JUST DROP OUT FROM UNDER YOU...
I'M ASKING, AND I REALLY WANT TO KNOW. HOW ARE YOU?
DO YOU EAT PANCAKES?
OH, I MEAN... I GUESS?
LET'S GET YOU SOME PANCAKES.

MARNIE'S
OPEN
THEY'RE GOOD.
I WOULDN'T TAKE YOU FOR SHITTY PANCAKES. I RESPECT MY TIME.
I SINCERELY THOUGHT YOU WERE GOING TO KILL ME THIS TIME.
DON'T PUSH IT, KID.
I BROUGHT YOU HERE BECAUSE YOU JUST GOT DROPPED IN THE DEEP END, AND I'M GIVING YOU A CHANCE TO ASK ME ALL THE SHIT YOU WANT TO ASK, BUT KNOW YOU PROBABLY CAN'T ON THE JOB.
HEH.
WHAT?
IT'S FUNNY. I'M SURE THAT'S WHAT EVERYONE ELSE WANTS WHEN YOU RECRUIT. THEY JUST SIGNED UP WITH THE DEPARTMENT OF TRUTH, AND NOW THEY WANT THE **REAL** ANSWERS.
BUT THERE AREN'T ANY. ISN'T THAT THE POINT?
YES. BUT PEOPLE ARE STUPID, SO THEY STILL HAVE QUESTIONS. AND I'M SURE YOU DO, TOO.

I SAW A LITERAL ICE WALL AT THE END OF THE WORLD, RUBY. I SAW PROOF THAT STANLEY KUBRICK FAKED THE MOON LANDING. I **KNOW** THE ANSWER TO EACH OF MY QUESTIONS.
COLLECTIVE BELIEF SHAPES THE WORLD, SO EVERYTHING IS A LITTLE BIT TRUE, OR HAS THE POTENTIAL TO BE TRUE.
ARE THERE ALIENS IN AREA 51? I'M SURE THERE ARE, OR THERE WERE, OR THERE **SOMETIMES** ARE DEPENDING ON WHICH MOVIES CAME OUT THAT YEAR.
MY HUSBAND WAS JOKING ABOUT REPTILIANS EARLIER.
I BET YOU'VE SEEN THEM WITH YOUR OWN EYES.
DAMN HARD TO KILL.
WAS THERE SOMEONE ON THE GRASSY KNOLL? THAT ONE IS HARDER.
IT IS, AND IT ISN'T.
BUT THAT'S NOT MY STORY TO TELL.

YOU THINK IT'S REALLY HIM? THAT THE DIRECTOR IS REALLY LEE HARVEY OSWALD? THE LEE HARVEY OSWALD?
THAT'S A GOOD WAY OF PHRASING IT. THE QUESTION IS WHICH OSWALD WAS HE? IS HE THE OSWALD WHO SHOT JFK? IS HE THE PATSY?
HE'S PROBABLY NOT THE ONE KILLED BY JACK RUBY.
ON THAT NOTE, I DON'T THINK I'M PAID TO BELIEVE IN COINCIDENCE ANYMORE. YOU'RE GOING TO HAVE TO TELL ME YOUR REAL NAME ONE OF THESE DAYS.
I DON'T HAVE TO DO A DAMN THING I DON'T WANT TO. I JUST BOUGHT YOU PANCAKES.
FAIR.
YOU'RE HANDLING ALL OF THIS WELL.
THE CORE CONCEIT OF IT ALL...THAT I CAN GRASP. THAT I UNDERSTAND.
IN THE ABSTRACT, IT MAKES PERFECT SENSE. THE PROBLEM IS WHERE IT GETS PERSONAL.
SATANIC PANIC.

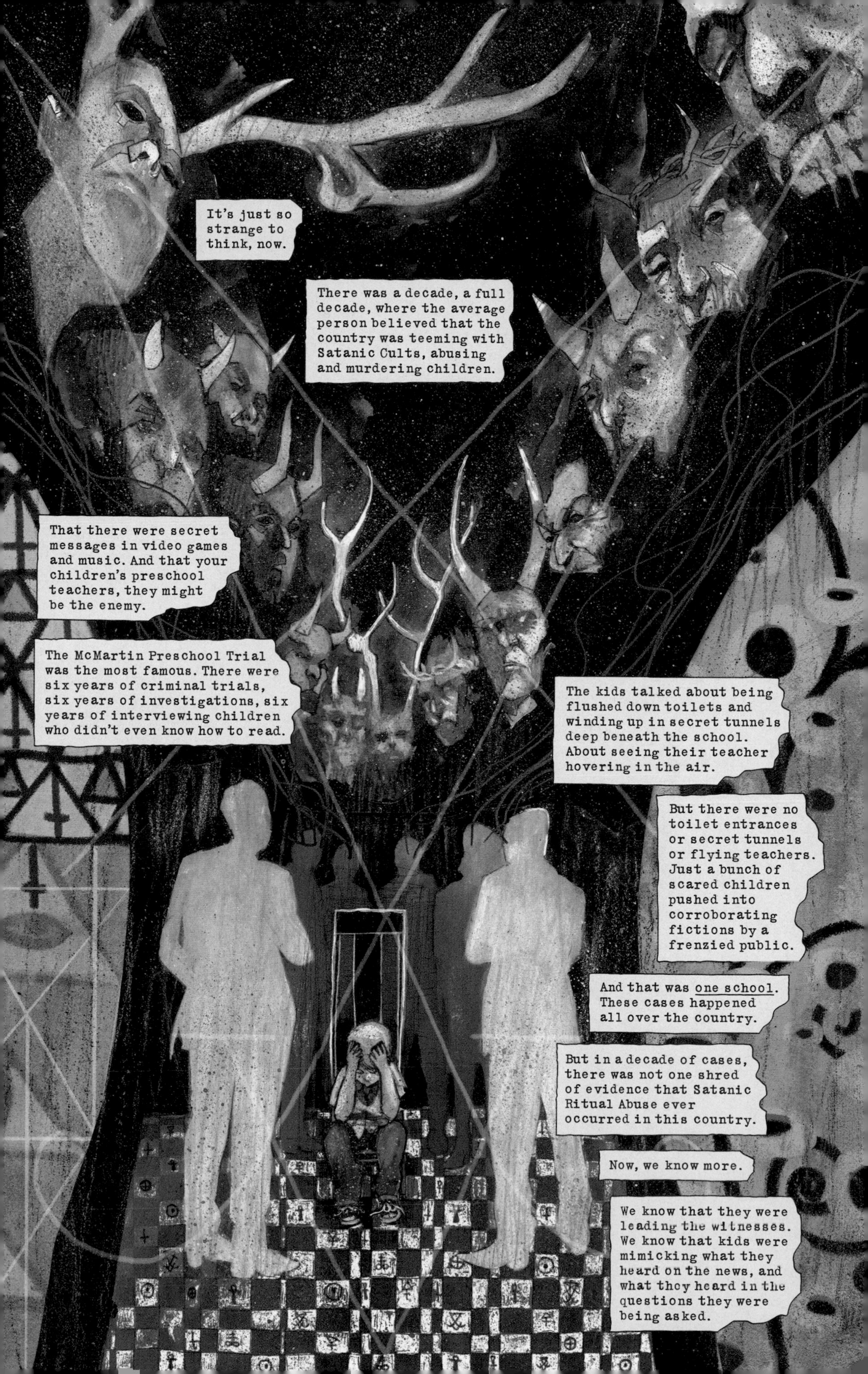
It's just so strange to think, now.
There was a decade, a full decade, where the average person believed that the country was teeming with Satanic Cults, abusing and murdering children.
That there were secret messages in video games and music. And that your children's preschool teachers, they might be the enemy.
The McMartin Preschool Trial was the most famous. There were six years of criminal trials, six years of investigations, six years of interviewing children who didn't even know how to read.
The kids talked about being flushed down toilets and winding up in secret tunnels deep beneath the school. About seeing their teacher hovering in the air.
But there were no toilet entrances or secret tunnels or flying teachers. Just a bunch of scared children pushed into corroborating fictions by a frenzied public.
And that was one school. These cases happened all over the country.
But in a decade of cases, there was not one shred of evidence that Satanic Ritual Abuse ever occurred in this country.
Now, we know more.
We know that they were leading the witnesses. We know that kids were mimicking what they heard on the news, and what they heard in the questions they were being asked.

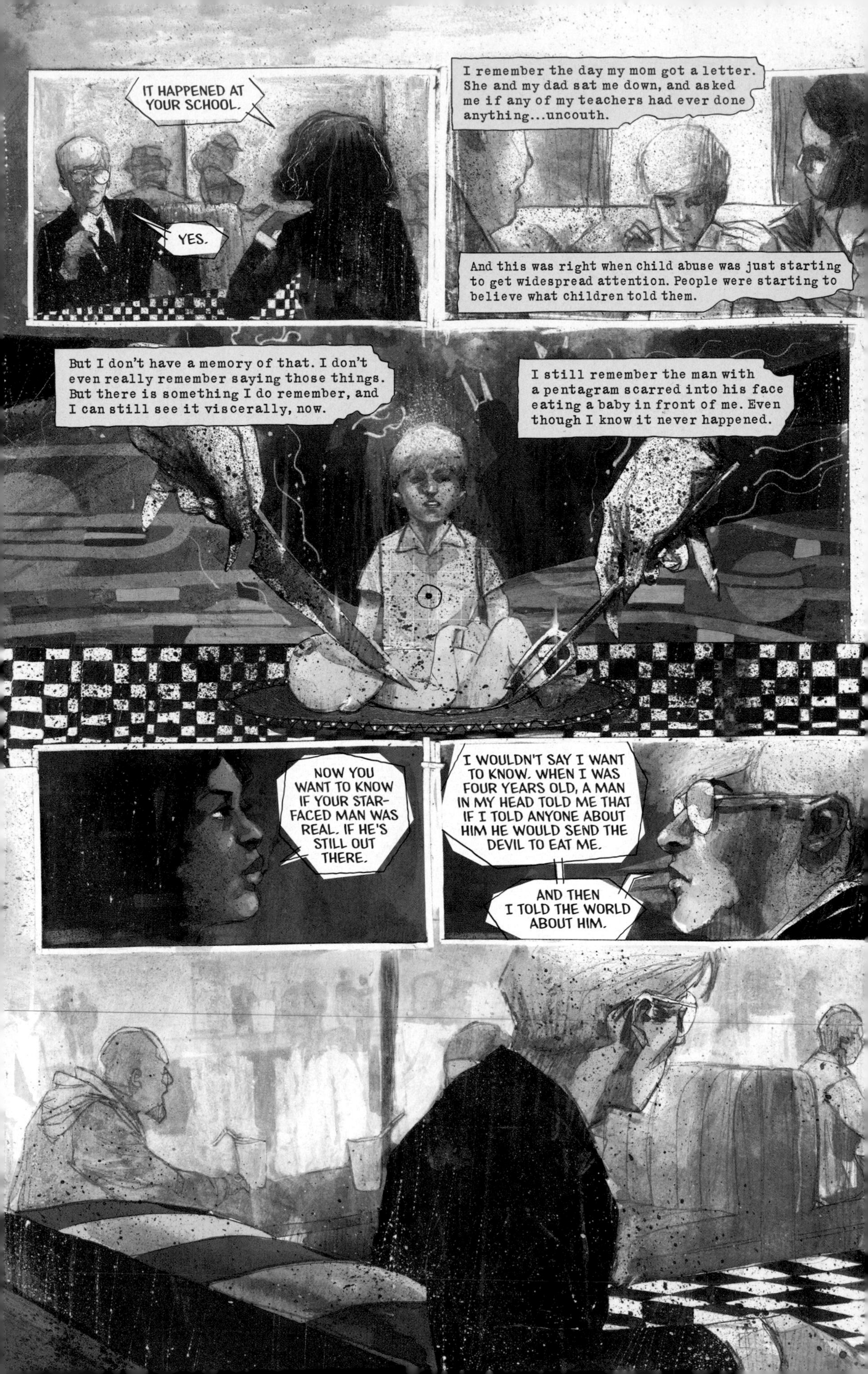
IT HAPPENED AT YOUR SCHOOL.
YES.
I remember the day my mom got a letter. She and my dad sat me down, and asked me if any of my teachers had ever done anything...uncouth.
And this was right when child abuse was just starting to get widespread attention. People were starting to believe what children told them.
But I don't have a memory of that. I don't even really remember saying those things. But there is something I do remember, and I can still see it viscerally, now.
I still remember the man with a pentagram scarred into his face eating a baby in front of me. Even though I know it never happened.
NOW YOU WANT TO KNOW IF YOUR STAR-FACED MAN WAS REAL. IF HE'S STILL OUT THERE.
I WOULDN'T SAY I WANT TO KNOW. WHEN I WAS FOUR YEARS OLD, A MAN IN MY HEAD TOLD ME THAT IF I TOLD ANYONE ABOUT HIM HE WOULD SEND THE DEVIL TO EAT ME.
AND THEN I TOLD THE WORLD ABOUT HIM.

And...Look...I still have the transcripts. I know everything I said. I don't know that we got much national attention, but it was all over the news in the upper Midwest.
My version of the toilets was a secret passage behind the bookcase where they kept the Play-Doh. And I talked about seeing my teachers eating other kids, and making us eat them.
When I had the dreams in the past, I knew I could go through the facts. I could assure myself that this never happened.
That it was a nightmare pried out of me by unscrupulous lawyers and psychologists.
BUT NOW...
I DON'T WANT TO KNOW, RUBY. I NEED TO KNOW.
OKAY, THEN.
IT'S TIME TO HIT ROCK BOTTOM.

DING
HOW MANY SUB-BASEMENTS ARE THERE IN THE BUILDING?
TWELVE I KNOW ABOUT.
BUT THIS IS THE DEEPEST I HAVE ACCESS TO.
ROCK BOTTOM.
YEAH.
IT SMELLS.
WE DON'T LET THEM OUT MUCH.
ARCHIVES
RUBY, IS THAT YOU?
HEY, HUNKY. I BROUGHT YOU PANCAKES.
CHOCOLATE CHIP?
OF COURSE.
THAT'S WHY I LOVE YOU. THEY SHOULD PUT YOU ON MONEY, AND WORSHIP YOU IN TEMPLES.

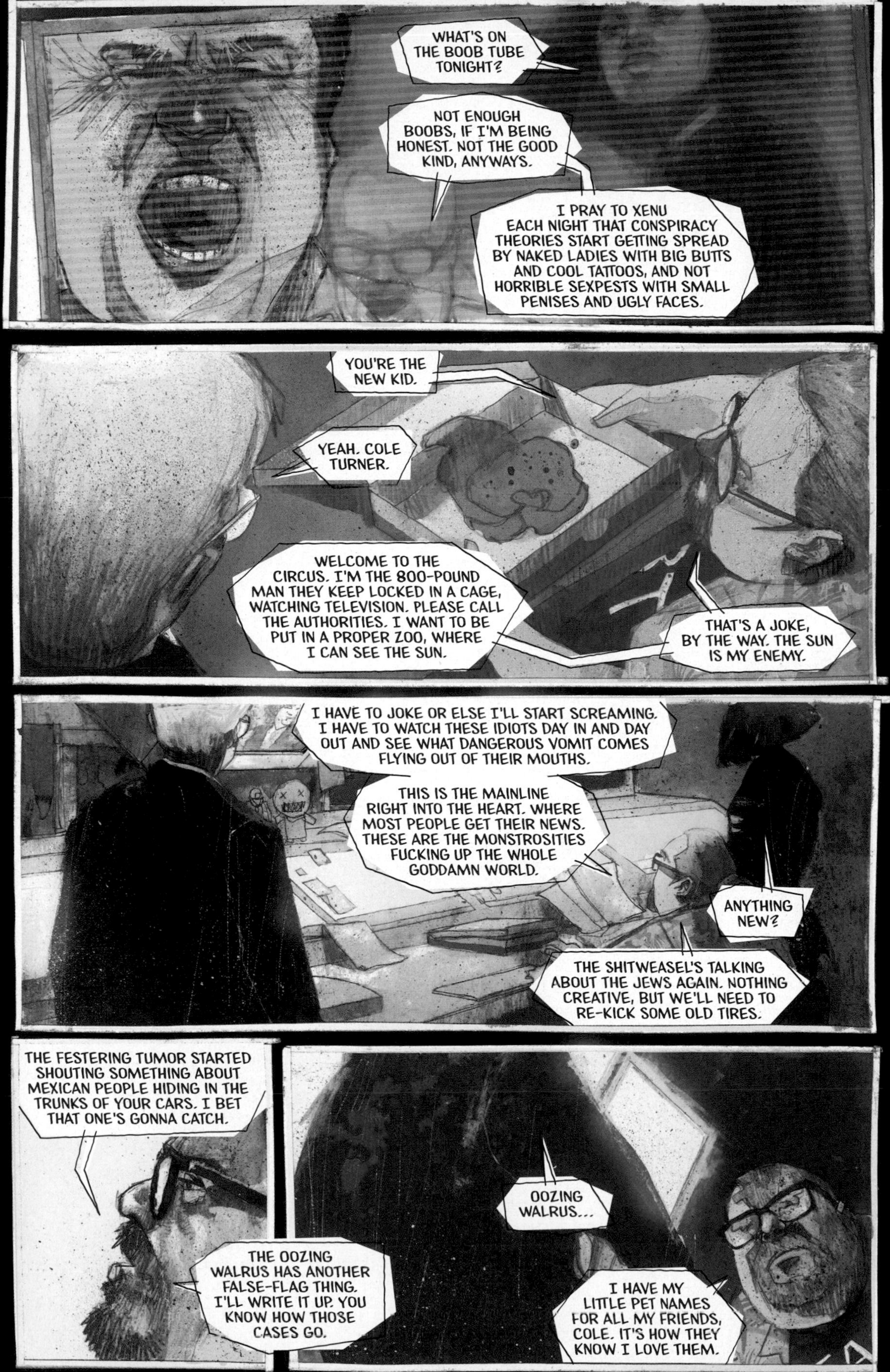
WHAT'S ON THE BOOB TUBE TONIGHT?
NOT ENOUGH BOOBS, IF I'M BEING HONEST. NOT THE GOOD KIND, ANYWAYS.
I PRAY TO XENU EACH NIGHT THAT CONSPIRACY THEORIES START GETTING SPREAD BY NAKED LADIES WITH BIG BUTTS AND COOL TATTOOS, AND NOT HORRIBLE SEXPESTS WITH SMALL PENISES AND UGLY FACES.
YOU'RE THE NEW KID.
YEAH. COLE TURNER.
WELCOME TO THE CIRCUS. I'M THE 800-POUND MAN THEY KEEP LOCKED IN A CAGE, WATCHING TELEVISION. PLEASE CALL THE AUTHORITIES. I WANT TO BE PUT IN A PROPER ZOO, WHERE I CAN SEE THE SUN.
THAT'S A JOKE, BY THE WAY. THE SUN IS MY ENEMY.
I HAVE TO JOKE OR ELSE I'LL START SCREAMING. I HAVE TO WATCH THESE IDIOTS DAY IN AND DAY OUT AND SEE WHAT DANGEROUS VOMIT COMES FLYING OUT OF THEIR MOUTHS.
THIS IS THE MAINLINE RIGHT INTO THE HEART. WHERE MOST PEOPLE GET THEIR NEWS. THESE ARE THE MONSTROSITIES FUCKING UP THE WHOLE GODDAMN WORLD.
ANYTHING NEW?
THE SHITWEASEL'S TALKING ABOUT THE JEWS AGAIN. NOTHING CREATIVE, BUT WE'LL NEED TO RE-KICK SOME OLD TIRES.
THE FESTERING TUMOR STARTED SHOUTING SOMETHING ABOUT MEXICAN PEOPLE HIDING IN THE TRUNKS OF YOUR CARS. I BET THAT ONE'S GONNA CATCH.
THE OOZING WALRUS HAS ANOTHER FALSE-FLAG THING. I'LL WRITE IT UP. YOU KNOW HOW THOSE CASES GO.
OOZING WALRUS...
I HAVE MY LITTLE PET NAMES FOR ALL MY FRIENDS, COLE. IT'S HOW THEY KNOW I LOVE THEM.

ANYTHING ON SATAN? SATANIC RITUAL ABUSE.
YOU WANT TO TALK ABOUT THE '80S. I LOVE THE '80S. BUT NOT MY AREA.
YOU'RE GOING TO WANT DOCTOR TIN-FOIL.
IF EITHER OF YOU WERE IN THIS DEPARTMENT IN THE '70S, YOU WOULDN'T BE LAUGHING AT MY HAT.
AND IT'S **STILL** IN THE MEDIA. IT MIGHT BE A JOKE, BUT THERE'S STILL AN UNDERLYING BELIEF STRUCTURE.
IF YOU WANT THE ENEMY TO RIP ALL OF THESE FLIPPING SECRETS OUT OF YOUR HEAD, YOU CAN BE MY GUEST.
DOC. THE NEW KID WANTS TO KNOW ABOUT ANY CONSISTENT FIGURES IN SATANIC RITUAL ABUSE CASES. ONES THAT MIGHT HAVE STEPPED OUT OF THE STORIES.
OH, OH SURE. SATANIC PANIC. THAT HAS ITS OWN ROOM IN THE BACK.
THIS IS HOW YOU KEEP THE ARCHIVES?
YES, I DEVELOPED THE SYSTEM BACK IN THE LATE '60S WITH LEE. WILD TIMES. COLD WAR WAS IN PLAY, AND YOU NEVER KNEW WHEN A NEWSPAPER MIGHT HAVE SECRET MESSAGES.
AND YOU DIDN'T DIGITIZE...
DIGITAL MEDIA CHANGES TOO QUICK. IT'S SO REACTIVE. YOU NEVER KNOW WHICH CHANGES HIT WIKIPEDIA BECAUSE PEOPLE'S BELIEFS SHIFT, OR IF IT'S ALL JUST A NO-GOOD TEENAGER.
AND THOSE MACHINES ARE TRYING TO REPROGRAM YOUR MINDS. THEY'RE SUCCEEDING, TOO. I LET THE KID DEAL WITH ALL OF THAT.
THE KID?
UP ON YOUR LEFT...

SAY HI, FRANK.
SHE SEEMS NICE.
THAT IS HER BEING NICE. YOU SHOULD SEE HER WHEN SHE'S SOBER.
I'M GOING TO BE ASKING YOU FOR A DEBRIEF SOON, HELP UPDATE MY ROOMS ON FLAT EARTH AND THE MOON LANDING.
NEVER THOUGHT THE FLAT EARTHERS WOULD SUBSUME THE MOON TRUTHERS, BUT THIS IS A WILD WORLD, ISN'T IT?
I'M GOING TO NEED MORE STRING. MAYBE TAKE DOWN A WALL.

OKAY, HERE. SATANIC PANIC.
DARK STUFF. I HATE WHEN KIDS GET DRAGGED INTO ALL OF THIS. THEY'RE SO PLIABLE, THEY BELIEVE SO READILY. I MEAN HECK, IF THERE WERE ENOUGH KIDS IN THE WORLD, WE'D HAVE TO GO KILL SANTA CLAUS EVERY YEAR.
THANKFULLY, THAT'S ONLY HAD TO HAPPEN ONCE OR TWICE.
IT'S A CYCLICAL THING. IT HAPPENS IN TIMES OF PRIMAL CULTURAL FEAR. SOME CHRISTIANS BELIEVED THAT JEWS WERE EATING THEIR BABIES UP UNTIL THE EARLY 20TH CENTURY. THAT WAS THE PRIMARY MODE OF THIS THEORY FOR A LONG TIME.
MORE RECENTLY IT'S DEMOCRATS. PIZZAGATE AND THE LIKE. BUT THERE'S STILL A RESIDUAL SATANIC IMPRINT ON THE CONCEPT. RITUAL PEDOPHILIA AS AN AFFRONT TO A CHRISTIAN GOD.
YOU WERE ASKING ABOUT A SINGULAR FIGURE...AND THERE ISN'T ONE. I THINK ANTON LAVEY HELPED SHAPE THE MODERN IMAGE OF A SATANIST IN POPULAR CULTURE, AND THERE ARE LITTLE TAGS, BUT THE SYMBOLS ARE JUMBLED TOGETHER...
WITHOUT ANYONE EVER CONVICTED FOR RITUAL ABUSE...THERE WASN'T ANYONE THE PUBLIC COULD SINK THEIR CLAWS INTO. NO ONE SPECIFIC FOR OUR DEPARTMENT TO GO AND SHUT DOWN.
I'M SORRY, DOC...
WHAT YEAR IS THIS PICTURE FROM?
PLEASE DON'T REMOVE ANY PINS FROM THE WALLS. THIS IS AN INTRICATE SYSTEM, AND ANY INTERFERENCE...

WHAT YEAR?!
THIS IS FROM LAST YEAR. WHY?
IT'S OKAY, COLE. NONE OF THIS IS REAL.
COLE, IS THAT...?
YES.
DO YOU HAVE TRANSCRIPTS FROM THIS KID'S FILE? WERE THEY INTERVIEWED?
I...I CAN LOOK.

HE SAID... IT WAS OKAY... HE SAID IT WASN'T REAL.
IT'S OKAY, CARRIE...
HE...HE SAID THE DEVIL WAS THERE. THAT SHE WAS WATCHING ME...
SHE...SHE WAS WEARING A RED DRESS.
AND HER EYES...SHE DIDN'T HAVE REAL EYES.

BUT HE... BUT HE WAS EATING THE BABY.
AND THEN... AND THEN SHE STEPPED OUT OF THE SHADOWS.
BUT SHE COULD SEE ME.
AND SHE WAS SMILING.

NO...
SHIT... COLE.
IT'S OKAY, COLE. NONE OF THIS IS REAL.
DOC, GET LEE...HE'S HAVING A BREAK.
NO! I WANT TO WAKE UP!
DID YOU SEE? IT'S IMPORTANT THAT YOU SEE.
I WANT TO WAKE UP!!

DEPARTMEN
UNITED STATE

CHAPTER 3 /

She remembers the first time she watched one of the videos. She remembers the man's red face, his jowls, his spittle, and his rage.
She had started getting angry messages mixed in with the condolences. She thought it was a joke at first. How could anyone not believe the shooting was real?
The image of the classroom door riddled with bullet holes was shown by every cable news channel for weeks. She had heard the gunshots herself, on a message from her son.
Him crying, begging for her to come save him. She had listened over and over to the bullets as they ripped her son's life away, and this sweating hog of a man was saying it hadn't happened? That it was a hoax?
She remembers laughing as she finished the video. She couldn't help herself.
She was comforted knowing that no one could possibly believe it.

NRA
GET YOUR HANDS OFF MY GUNS

THEY ARE COMING, MARK MY WORDS. THEY'LL PULL EVERY TRICK IN THE BOOK TO STRIP DOWN YOUR ARSENAL, AND THEN THEY'LL COME!
AND WHAT? YOU'LL FIGHT OFF THEIR DRONE MISSILES WITH STICKS?! NO! YOU'LL NEED THE HEAVY ARTILLERY!
THIS IS YOUR GOD-DAMNED COUNTRY! THESE ARE YOUR GOD-DAMNED RIGHTS!
YOU BEEN DRINKING, MARY? YOU DON'T SEEM YOURSELF.
OH, NO. I'M JUST FINE.
DID YOU TALK TO THE PEOPLE IN THE CAR?

IT'S LIKE I SAID BEFORE, MARY. THEY'RE FROM THE ELECTRIC COMPANY.
THEY DON'T LOOK LIKE IT.
I CALLED IT IN, AND THEY SAY IT'S LEGIT. BUT YOU KNOW YOU CAN CALL ME HERE IF YOU DON'T FEEL SAFE, OKAY? I CAN BE AT YOUR DOOR IN JUST A COUPLE OF MINUTES.
I'M SURE IT'S FINE, THEN.
NO ONE IS GOING TO FIGHT FOR YOU! IF YOU'RE A REAL AMERICAN, YOU HAVE TO FIGHT FOR YOURSELF!
SECURITY

CHAPTER THREE
BLACK AND WHITE

She had never heard the phrase *"false flag"* before the video. She had to google it.
It had once been the term they used to refer to a ship flying the flag of their opponent to sneak behind enemy lines. Now it was mostly used in the strange corners of the internet.
People claimed that left wing groups and the media were paying *"crisis actors"* to fake a rise in gun violence against children across the country.
They believed that this would create the groundswell of support the government needed to step in and take the guns of everyday honest Americans.
There were pictures of her and her son on message boards. Long threads comparing her boy to child actors from commercials filmed years ago, trying to prove their case.
One of the forums found her personal email. The messages started, calling her a liar and a government stooge. A profiteer who didn't care about her country, seeking fame by crying in front of the cameras.
And then the calls started, on her cell, and her landline.
One night she saw an obese man in a track suit standing across the street from her house.
She kept her lights out that night, kneeling close to the window, watching him back, trying to decide whether or not to call the police.
He left shortly before daybreak.

She couldn't afford the house in the gated community, but she didn't think there was really any choice after the third brick flew through her front window.
Her father gave her the money he had saved for his grandson's college fund to help with the down payment.
At night she played the message, over and over again. Listening to the sound of her ten-year-old son, sobbing for his mom to come save him.
Listening to the sound of the bullets, and his slow death rattle. She hadn't picked up the phone over her lunch break.
She can't remember if she ignored the call, or truly didn't hear it ringing. It's not that picking up would have changed the outcome, but at least the last sounds he heard would have been his mother telling him she loved him.

"They don't look real at all," she said. "It looks like she doesn't feel anything."
And she'd agree with the comments about whether her tears looked real or not on the news channel.
She even responded to some of the pictures of child actors they posted. "No, the eyebrows aren't right," she'd add to the thread.
She thought about killing herself, but she didn't want to put her father out any further. So instead, she read through the bile and the hate.
The day after the shooting, she had wondered if she would become an alcoholic, but there didn't seem to be an amount of liquor that made her feel drunk anymore.

THIS IS FASCINATING. SHE HAS PRINTOUTS OF THE ENTIRE SCHOOL. MINUTES OF THE SHOOTING FROM THE POLICE.
I THINK THIS PIN IS MEANT TO REPRESENT HER SON, ROGER.
QUIET, COLE.
I ALREADY CHECKED ON HER UPSTAIRS. SHE'S OUT.
HM.

SHIT.
WHAT IS IT?
THIS IS BAD. SHE ALREADY GOT HER HANDS ON THE ARTIFACT.
BLACK HAT...
RUBY!
SHE'S *BEHIND* YOU!
I SAID, **QUIET!**
SIT DOWN.
YEAH. OKAY.

She had found the envelope on her doorstep. She didn't know how long it had been there. She hadn't left the house for days.
She phoned the gatehouse, but the guard seemed exhausted by her before she even got the question out.
She hung up without an answer and took the envelope into her living room. Inside was a small flash drive.
The drive made her feel as if she was going to vomit, though she couldn't say why. There was a large part of her that just wanted to drop it in the garbage disposal.
But instead, she connected it to her laptop, and began to play the video she found inside.

MOMMY...MOMMY, ARE YOU THERE? PLEASE... I WANT TO GO HOME. I WANT TO GO HOME, MOMMY. PLEASE. PLEASE LET ME COME HOME.
AND THEN THERE'S THE GUNFIRE. BLAM BLAM BLAM.
BLAM.
HAHAHAHA...
HE CAN DO IT AGAIN FROM THE TOP, IF YOU WANT. I THINK HE GOT THE CRYING DOWN A BIT BETTER ON THE DRIVE OVER.
OH, DON'T YOU WORRY, MS. TODD. I THINK YOU AND YOUR BOY ARE A NATURAL FIT FOR OUR PROJECT. NOW, ARE YOU COMFORTABLE WITH BEING ON THE NEWS? SPEAKING TO REPORTERS?
YES. I'VE BEEN TAKING IMPROV CLASSES LIKE YOU SUGGESTED. I DIDN'T USE MY REAL NAME. BUT I THINK I'LL BE READY.
She didn't finish the video that first time.
She couldn't bring herself to do it. She just paused it, and stared at herself until the computer died on the kitchen table.
She didn't know if she was going to scream or throw up. When she finally willed herself to move, she played the message from her son, from the shooting.
Every word he said matched the video.
He had been reading a script.
It took her another six hours to admit to herself that, if this video was real, that meant her son was still alive.

I KNOW YOU'RE NOT FROM THE ELECTRIC COMPANY.
OKAY. YEAH. I'M NOT FROM THE ELECTRIC COMPANY.
I WANT TO KNOW WHERE MY SON IS.
YOUR SON?
DON'T BULLSHIT ME!! I KNOW WHO YOU ARE!! I KNOW WHO SENT YOU!
NO! NO, HE ISN'T! NO, HE FUCKING ISN'T!
WE WENT TO THE GRAVEYARD BEFORE WE CAME HERE, MARY. WE EXHUMED THE BODY, TO MAKE SURE... THAT HE WAS STILL THERE.
YOU...WHAT DID YOU DO?

WHO DO YOU THINK SENT US?
YOU'RE... YOU'RE JUST TRYING TO CONFUSE ME!
I PROMISE THAT'S NOT WHAT I'M DOING. THAT'S NOT WHAT I CAME HERE TO DO.
I'M NOT GOING TO JUST LET YOU KILL ME! NOT WHEN I KNOW ROGER IS STILL OUT THERE.
I'M SORRY, MARY. YOUR SON IS DEAD. HE AND FOURTEEN OTHER KIDS WERE SHOT AND KILLED LATE LAST YEAR.
FOR THE LOVE OF GOD, COLE, YOU NEED TO SHUT THE FUCK UP.

She bought a printer and paper at the local office supply store.
The men on those forums had gathered so much evidence already. Some of it was noise, but some of it started to worm into the back of her mind.
There was a video online of an improv team's class performance down in the city, and she couldn't help but notice that the woman looked remarkably like herself.
If she pulled her hair back and wore glasses, and had a tattoo on her arm ... But all of those things could be faked so easily.
She started asking in each of the forums where they thought the children were being kept. Did they think the children were safe? The answers only made her feel worse.
One man wrote a long post about how the children were being sold into sexual slavery to Democratic congressmen, and she couldn't let herself even entertain that.
She pictured her boy in some kind of boarding school, under some false name, laughing and playing with friends.

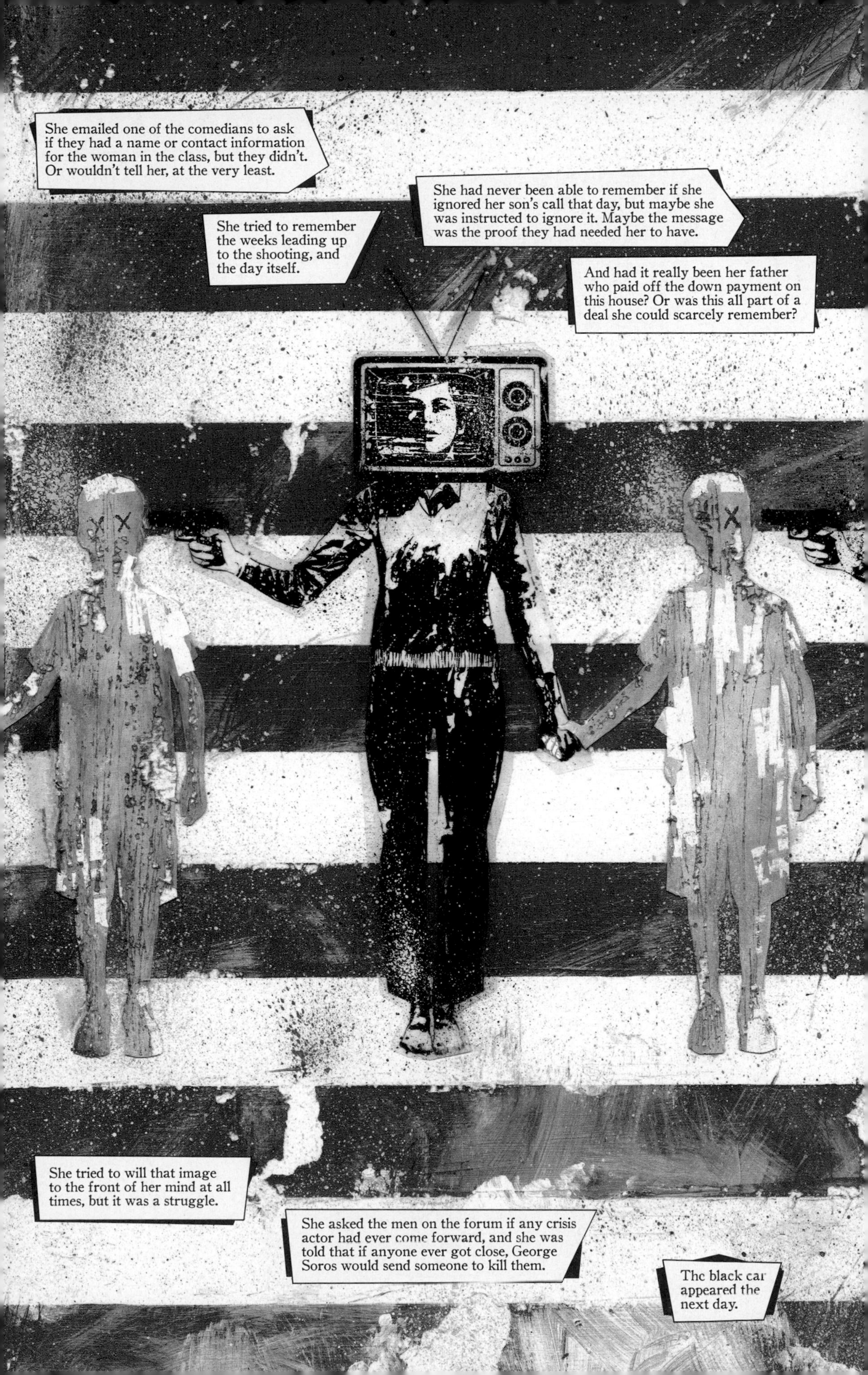
She emailed one of the comedians to ask if they had a name or contact information for the woman in the class, but they didn't. Or wouldn't tell her, at the very least.
She tried to remember the weeks leading up to the shooting, and the day itself.
She had never been able to remember if she ignored her son's call that day, but maybe she was instructed to ignore it. Maybe the message was the proof they had needed her to have.
And had it really been her father who paid off the down payment on this house? Or was this all part of a deal she could scarcely remember?
She tried to will that image to the front of her mind at all times, but it was a struggle.
She asked the men on the forum if any crisis actor had ever come forward, and she was told that if anyone ever got close, George Soros would send someone to kill them.
The black car appeared the next day.

SO...WHAT HAPPENS NOW?
WE DESTROY THE VIDEO AND THE FLASH DRIVE. IT GOES BACK TO BEING FICTION. SHE NEVER POSTS IT ONLINE. SHE NEVER COMES FORWARD WITH "PROOF" THAT THE SHOOTING DIDN'T HAPPEN.
"CRISIS ACTORS" REMAIN A FRINGE THEORY UNTIL THE NEXT TIME WE NEED TO SHUT ONE OF THESE DOWN.
AND HER SON STAYS DEAD.
THERE'S NO GUARANTEE THAT THE BOY WOULD BE ALIVE EVEN IF THAT THEORY TOOK HOLD.
HE COULD HAVE BEEN KILLED TO KEEP THE WHOLE OPERATION QUIET. THERE ARE A MILLION DIFFERENT WAYS IT COULD HAVE GONE WRONG.
IT STILL FEELS OFF.
LIKE WE JUST TOOK HIM FROM HER AGAIN. THE CHANCE THAT HE'S STILL OUT THERE. WHAT DOES SHE EVEN DO WITH ALL OF THIS? WILL SHE JUST FORGET?
YEAH.

WE AREN'T THE MEN IN BLACK. THERE AREN'T NEURALYZERS.
SO WHAT HAPPENS TO HER?
HOPEFULLY... SHE SLEEPS FOR A LONG TIME. LONGER THAN SHE HAS IN MONTHS. AND HER BRAIN TREATS ALL OF THIS AS SOME KIND OF DREAM.
AND IF IT DOESN'T?
THEN SHE'LL SPEND THE REST OF HER LIFE BELIEVING THAT AGENTS OF GEORGE SOROS TOOK AWAY THE ONLY PROOF THAT HER SON WAS ALIVE.
BUT WITHOUT THAT PROOF, EVERY-ONE WILL JUST THINK SHE'S CRAZY.
AND YOU'RE OKAY WITH THAT?
THIS ISN'T A CLEAN JOB, COLE. IT'S UGLY. BECAUSE PEOPLE ARE UGLY, AND THEY CAN BELIEVE TERRIBLE, UGLY THINGS.
I SLEEP FINE. ALRIGHT?
YEAH. ALRIGHT.

SO, BLACK HAT. TELL ME ABOUT THEM.
I DON'T KNOW MUCH MORE THAN YOU DO, COLE.
BUT YOU'RE SCARED OF THEM.
IN THE LAST MONTH, THEY HELPED MANIFEST A LITERAL WALL AT THE END OF THE WORLD AND SENT THIS WOMAN A VIDEO OF THINGS THAT HAVE NEVER HAPPENED.
YEAH. I'M SCARED.
AND YOU SHOULD BE, TOO.

She knew what had happened before her eyes opened, before she could get herself down the stairs.
Her files were gone. The video was gone. All the work she'd done to connect the dots had been undone. Covered up.
She went to one of the forums, and began to type. Her fingers ached against the keyboard as she pounded sentences away, in red-faced fury.
She wrote that she had proof, but mysterious government agents had come into her house and taken it all away from her.
Her son was out there, somewhere, and the government was hiding him from her. He was still alive. She was a liar and she should go to jail, but her son should have his life back.
She caught her reflection in a mirror. She saw herself red-faced, and shaking. And mad.
And she saw the gun on the table. And the sight of it made her sick.

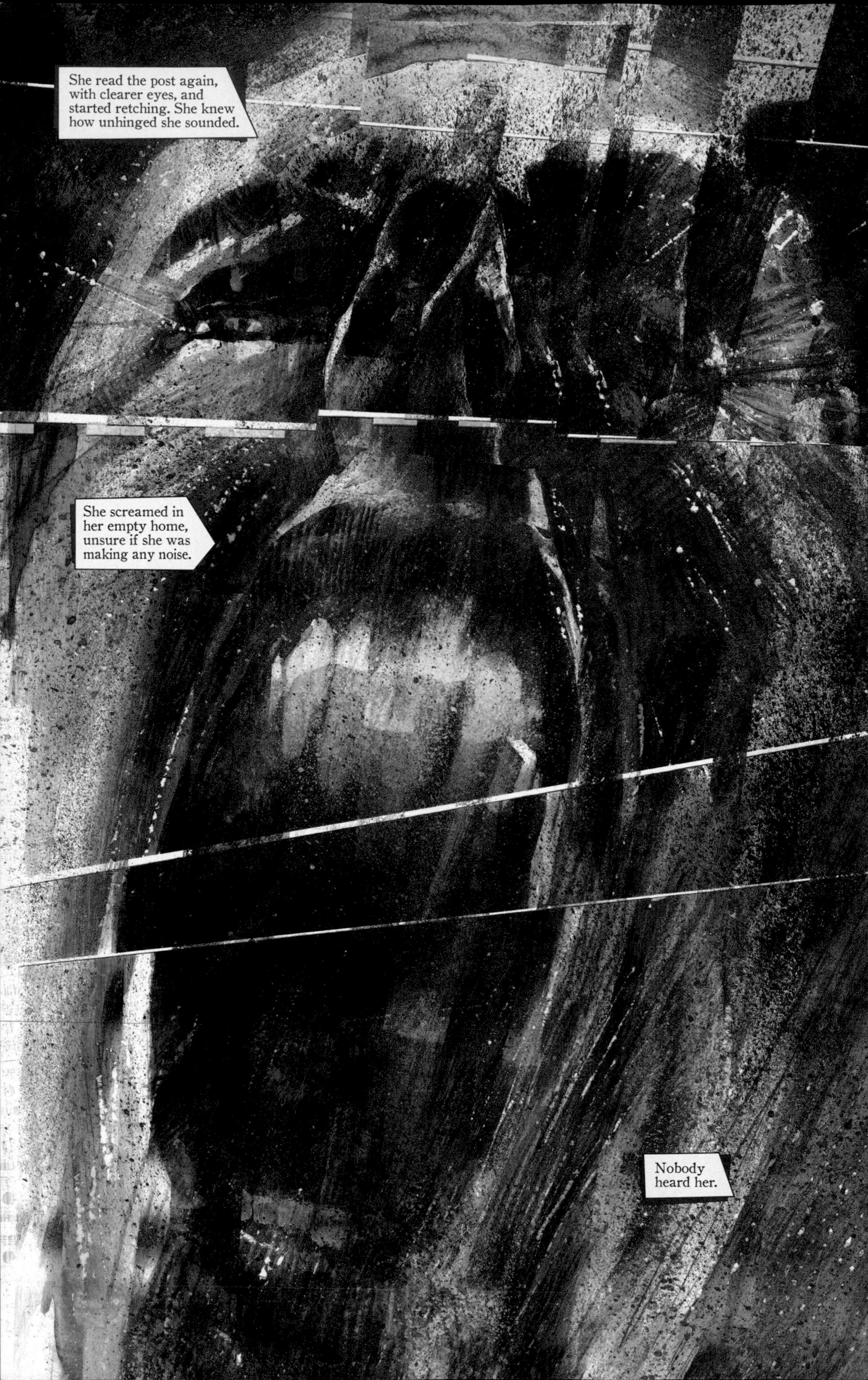
She read the post again, with clearer eyes, and started retching. She knew how unhinged she sounded.
She screamed in her empty home, unsure if she was making any noise.
Nobody heard her.

DEPARTMEN
UNITED STATE

CHAPTER 4

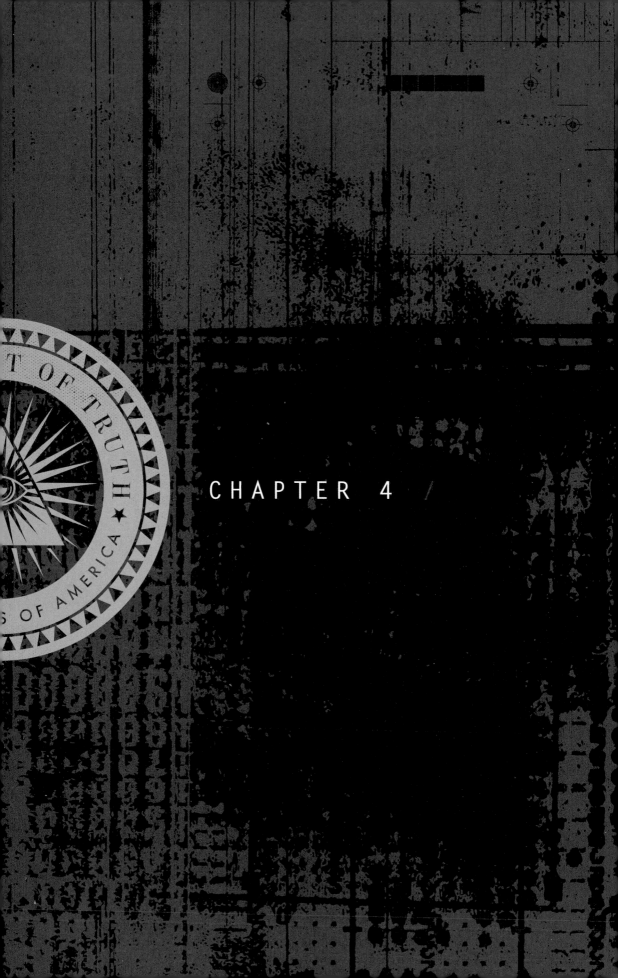

1910
1950
1970

22:0003656868
FUCK. I DON'T KNOW WHERE I WANT TO START.
22:0003656868 >>
YOU'RE SCARING ME, DAN.
I KNOW.
YOU'VE NEVER DROPPED OFF THE FACE OF THE EARTH LIKE THIS BEFORE.
I KNOW.
22:0003656868 >>
WHERE HAVE YOU BEEN? WHEN DID YOU SWITCH APARTMENTS?
CAMERA OFF
NONE OF THAT MATTERS, ROBBIE. ALL OF THAT IS JUST NOISE. I DID WHAT I THOUGHT I HAD TO, TO GET THE RIGHT PERSPECTIVE ON ALL OF THIS...IT DIDN'T WORK. THAT'S WHY I CALLED YOU.

22:00036568
TALK TO ME, DAN.
DO YOU EVER THINK ABOUT WHAT WE DO? NOT IN THE PRACTICAL SENSE. THE BIG PICTURE OF WHAT WE DO AS MEMBERS OF THE PRESS.
22:0003656868
WE'VE PUT ALL THESE AIRS ON IT. THE IDEA THAT WE'RE THIS NOBLE **FOURTH ESTATE,** A CHECK ON THE POWERFUL AND THE NOT-POWERFUL ALL AT ONCE.
BUT YOU KNOW DAMN WELL THAT WE'RE JUST FULL OF SHIT. WE'VE CREATED ALL THESE RULES AND ETHICS TO MASK WHAT WE'VE ALWAYS BEEN.
OUR PAPER IS OWNED BY THE RICHEST MAN IN THE **WORLD,** FOR GOD'S SAKE. HOW IS IT ANY DIFFERENT THAN IT WAS A CENTURY AGO WITH **HEARST** AND **PULITZER?!**
22:00036568
INFORMATION CAN BE SO FUCKING DANGEROUS. IT CAN DESTROY LIVES AND DESTABILIZE GOVERNMENTS, AND MORE OFTEN THAN NOT WE WIELD IT LIKE IDIOT CHILDREN.
OF **COURSE** YOU DO. YOU'RE A CYNICAL BASTARD.
I DON'T APPRECIATE YOUR TONE.
DON'T GIVE ME THIS...FUCK... THIS **PLAY-ACTING.** I NEED YOU TO STOP SAYING WHAT YOU THINK YOU'RE SUPPOSED TO SAY AND ACTUALLY LISTEN TO ME.
I NEED TO TELL YOU A STORY THAT NEVER HAPPENED. THAT COULDN'T HAVE HAPPENED.
BY THE ETHICS OF OUR PAPER, AND THE INSTITUTION OF THE PRESS, IT IS IMPORTANT THAT WE PUBLISH THIS STORY.
22:00036568
BUT WE **CAN'T.**

NO. THAT'S INCIDENTAL. THAT'S JUST, FUCK, I DON'T KNOW... THE LATEST VERSION OF A THING THAT HAS BEEN GROWING LIKE A TUMOR FOR THE LAST FIVE HUNDRED YEARS.
WE PUT OUT A DAILY NEWSPAPER THAT INFORMS MILLIONS--
SINCE GUTENBERG BUILT HIS PRINTING PRESS. SINCE INFORMATION BECAME SOMETHING YOU COULD SELL ON THE STREET TO ANYONE WHO COULD READ IT.
PEOPLE ARE HUNGRY FOR INFORMATION. THEY ARE RAVENOUS FOR IT, AND IT'S OUR JOB TO KEEP THEM FED.
IT DOESN'T MATTER WHAT INFORMATION IT IS, AS LONG AS WE GOT TO IT FIRST. WE'RE NOT THIS... VALIANT INSTITUTION.
RATHER THAN TREAT IT LIKE WHAT IT IS. A WEAPON.
22:0003656868 >>
I DON'T BELIEVE THAT.
I NEED YOU TO LOOK AT WHAT I HAVE HERE WITH CLEAN EYES AND A CLEAR HEAD SO YOU CAN HELP ME MAKE A DECISION.
WHAT THE HELL IS THIS ABOUT? WHAT ARE YOU TALKING ABOUT?
22:0003656868
WHAT IS THIS SYMBOL... THIS HAT?

22:0003656
I DON'T KNOW. THEY STARTED ARRIVING A FEW MONTHS AGO.
BUT I'M PRETTY SURE THEY'RE THE REASON WE'RE BEING LISTENED TO RIGHT NOW.
22:0003656868 >>
chapter four
THE EYES IN THE WALLS

I WANT A BETTER SHOT...HE KEEPS PACING AROUND LIKE A MANIAC..
I DON'T HAVE A DRONE IN THERE, LEE. THAT'S NOT HOW THIS WORKS.
WHAT FUCKING USE ARE THESE EXPENSIVE FUCKING TOYS IF THEY DON'T FUCKING WORK?
THEY DO WORK. YOU'RE JUST GRUMPY YOU DON'T UNDERSTAND HOW THEY WORK.
BACK IN THE DAY, WE USED TAPE.
DUCT TAPE.
IT WASN'T DUCT TAPE. IT WAS MAGNETIC TAPE.
LIKE A REFRIGERATOR MAGNET. GOT IT.
NO!
NOT LIKE A FUCKING--
HMPH.
YOU'RE JUST TRYING TO GET ME WORKED UP.

YEAH. I GET FIFTY BUCKS FROM HUNKY EVERY TIME I GET YOU TO YELL AT ME.
HOW ABOUT YOU GIVE ME A CUT OF THE ACTION, AND I CAN PUT ON A WHOLE SHOW. THROBBING VEIN ON THE FOREHEAD AND EVERYTHING.
I DON'T WANT TO HEAR ABOUT YOUR THROBBING VEINS, LEE.
HEY!
THAT WASN'T WHAT I--
OH.
FUCK.
YEAH. I'M GONNA BUY A CAR.
OOF.
UH, OKAY, I HAVE COFFEES.
I SPILLED A LITTLE ON MYSELF ON THE WAY UP. AND AGAIN, RIGHT THEN. BUT THEY'RE MOSTLY WHERE THEY SHOULD BE. IN THEIR CUPS.

THE GUY THOUGHT I WAS JOKING WHEN I ASKED FOR SIX SHOTS OF ESPRESSO WITH A SPLASH OF COFFEE.
MAMA NEEDS HER GASOLINE.
THIS PLACE IS INCREDIBLE. DO YOU LIVE HERE, DIRECTOR OSWALD?
DON'T BE STUPID. I LIVE SOMEWHERE NICE. NOT IN THE CITY.
AND DON'T DO THAT. JUST CALL ME LEE. THANKS FOR THE PICK-ME-UP. YOU CAN GO NOW.
GO?
LOOK. I'M NOT YOUR INTERN...
I HEAR YOU WERE CRYING IN THE FUCKING BASEMENT OVER SOME FAIRY TALE YOU COOKED UP AS A KID, AND THAT YOU ALMOST BUNGLED UP THE WHOLE SITUATION IN CONNECTICUT.
I NEEDED TO MAKE SURE YOU WERE HALFWAY WORTH A DAMN.
YOU DIDN'T FUCK UP THE COFFEE. SO, AT LEAST YOU HAVE THAT GOING FOR YOU.
TRY TO SPILL LESS OF IT ON YOURSELF NEXT TIME, AND I'LL CONSIDER PUTTING YOU ON ANOTHER FIELD JOB.

SIR...
JUST CALL ME LEE.
LEE.
YOU TOLD ME WHEN YOU HIRED ME THAT YOU WOULD LET ME ASK QUESTIONS.
OH, FOR THE LOVE OF GOD. YOUR GENERATION ARE A BUNCH OF SENSITIVE LITTLE FUCKING **BABIES,** AREN'T YOU?
I WANT TO BE ABLE TO START INVESTIGATING THE STAR-FACED MAN FULL-TIME. I WANT TO FIND HIM, AND ELIMINATE HIM BEFORE HE CAN HURT MORE CHILDREN.
ALL THESE THINGS ARE CONNECTED. YOU GET THAT, RIGHT?
THE FICTIONAL WOMAN WITH NO EYES. YOUR STAR-FACED MAN. THE BLACK HAT. THERE ARE FORCES OUT THERE WITH THEIR OWN AGENDA. WE ARE FIGHTING THAT AGENDA.
LEE...
YOU DIDN'T REALLY THINK I BROUGHT YOU HERE FOR COFFEE, DID YOU?
IF YOU WERE PAYING ATTENTION YOU'D KNOW THAT I'M ALREADY ANSWERING THOSE QUESTIONS.
NOW SHUT UP AND **LISTEN.**

YOU NEED TO UNDERSTAND WHAT WE DO, COLE. WHAT WE COMBAT. THE MOST DANGEROUS THING IN THE WORLD IS A SIMPLE STORY.
THAT'S WHAT KEEPS MOST CONSPIRACIES FROM CATCHING ON WITH THE GENERAL PUBLIC--THEY ARE TOO CONVOLUTED. CONVOLUTION IS OUR FRIEND.
IT HELPS FRACTURE BELIEF SO IT DOESN'T COALESCE IN ANY ONE STABLE FORM AND BECOME TRUTH.
LIKE WHO KILLED JFK.
THAT'S RIGHT. EXACTLY LIKE THAT. EVEN WHEN A MAJORITY BELIEVES THAT THERE WAS A CONSPIRACY, NOBODY CAN AGREE WHICH ONE WINS OUT.
THE MOB. THE CIA. THE CUBANS. A LONE GUNMAN. A MAGIC BULLET. THERE'S NO ONE ANSWER. NO FIRM BELIEF. JUST A BELIEF THAT THERE'S MORE TO THE STORY THAN THEY KNOW.
AND FUCK YOU VERY MUCH, BY THE WAY.
BUT OCCASIONALLY, A NARRATIVE HITS A NERVE, AND IT SPREADS. USUALLY BECAUSE THE GENERAL POPULACE IS UNCOMFORTABLE ABOUT SOME-THING.
LET'S SAY, FOR INSTANCE--AND I'M JUST PULLING THIS OUT OF MY ASS--LET'S SAY THEY'RE UNCOMFORTABLE WITH THE IDEA OF A BLACK PRESIDENT.

BARACK OBAMA CONTRADICTS THE IMAGE THEY HAVE IN THEIR HEAD FOR WHAT A PRESIDENT LOOKS LIKE AND SOUNDS LIKE, AND IT UNSETTLES THEM ON A SUBCONSCIOUS LEVEL.
AND THEN SOMEBODY PRESENTS AN ANSWER TO WHY THEY FEEL UNCOMFORTABLE. HE'S NOT FROM HERE. HE WASN'T BORN IN THIS COUNTRY, HE WAS BORN IN KENYA.
IT DOESN'T MATTER THAT YOU OR I CAN DISPROVE THAT THEORY SIX WAYS TO SUNDAY.
THERE'S A PART OF THEIR BRAINS THAT FEELS RELIEVED, BECAUSE THAT LIE GIVES THEM A SENSE OF ORDER.
THEY AREN'T BAD PEOPLE FOR FEELING UNSETTLED BY A BLACK PRESIDENT. THEY AREN'T RACIST. THEY'RE JUST SMART ENOUGH TO SEE THROUGH THE RUSE.
AND THAT'S WHEN THINGS GET VERY DANGEROUS FOR US.
BECAUSE THEY START BUILDING A WHOLE NEW TRUTH ON THE SIMPLE IDEA THAT OBAMA IS KENYAN. THEY START ASKING WHO WOULD ALLOW THAT TO HAPPEN AND WHAT THEY REALLY WANT.
EXACTLY.
SIX MONTHS AGO, THE REPORTER IN THAT APARTMENT WAS SENT A CLASSIFIED DOCUMENT SIGNED BY CIA DIRECTOR ALLEN DULLES IN 1961, ORDERING THE DESTRUCTION OF KENYAN BIRTH RECORDS FOR A BARACK HUSSEIN OBAMA II, AND THE CREATION OF NEW BIRTH RECORDS IN HAWAII.

22:00036568 >>
WHAT ARE YOU SAYING?
I'M NOT SAYING **ANYTHING,** ROBBIE.
WHO SENT YOU THIS?
22:00036568
ALL I HAVE IS THE SYMBOL. THE LITTLE BLACK HAT.
I'M NOT GOING TO SIT HERE AND LISTEN TO DERANGED CONSPIRACY THEORIES.
22:00036568
YES, YOU ARE. YOU **HAVE** TO. I NEED YOU TO SEE THE FULL PICTURE HERE.
22:00036568 >>
I THOUGHT DULLES WAS FIRED IN '61, AFTER THE BAY OF PIGS.
NOT UNTIL NOVEMBER, A FEW MONTHS AFTER THIS DOCUMENT WOULD HAVE BEEN SIGNED.
22:00036568
YOU SAID THIS WAS THE FIRST ENVELOPE. THE FIRST OF HOW MANY?

TWELVE.
THE FIRST ENVELOPE IS THE ORDER TO CHANGE OBAMA'S BIRTH LOCATION. AUGUST 1961.
THE SECOND IS THE RECORD OF A MEETING BETWEEN DULLES AND GEORGE H. W. BUSH IN HOUSTON, 1962, SHORTLY BEFORE BUSH RUNS FOR POLITICAL OFFICE THE FIRST TIME.
THE THIRD IS A REQUEST BY DULLES TO PULL A YOUNG TEENAGER NAMED WILLIAM JEFFERSON CLINTON FROM HIS WHITE HOUSE TRIP WITH BOYS NATION. JULY 1963.
THE SEVENTH IS A DEBRIEFING WITH CIA ASSET JEFFREY EPSTEIN, IN SAUDI ARABIA, REGARDING HIM RETURNING TO WASHINGTON TO THROW A PARTY FOR THE VICE-PRESIDENT AND OTHER PROMINENT POLITICIANS. 1983.
THE EIGHTH IS A DIRECTIVE FROM A MEMBER OF THE DEEP STATE COMMANDING PRESIDENT GEORGE H. W. BUSH TO SHIFT GEARS AND BEGIN CREATING A POST-SOVIET THREAT FOR THE AMERICAN PUBLIC IN THE MIDDLE EAST. 1990.
THE NINTH IS THE KILL ORDER FOR VINCE FOSTER AFTER HE THREATENED TO REVEAL A DECADENT PARTY WITH THE CLINTONS AND EPSTEIN, AND THE SATANIC ACTS PERFORMED THERE. 1993.

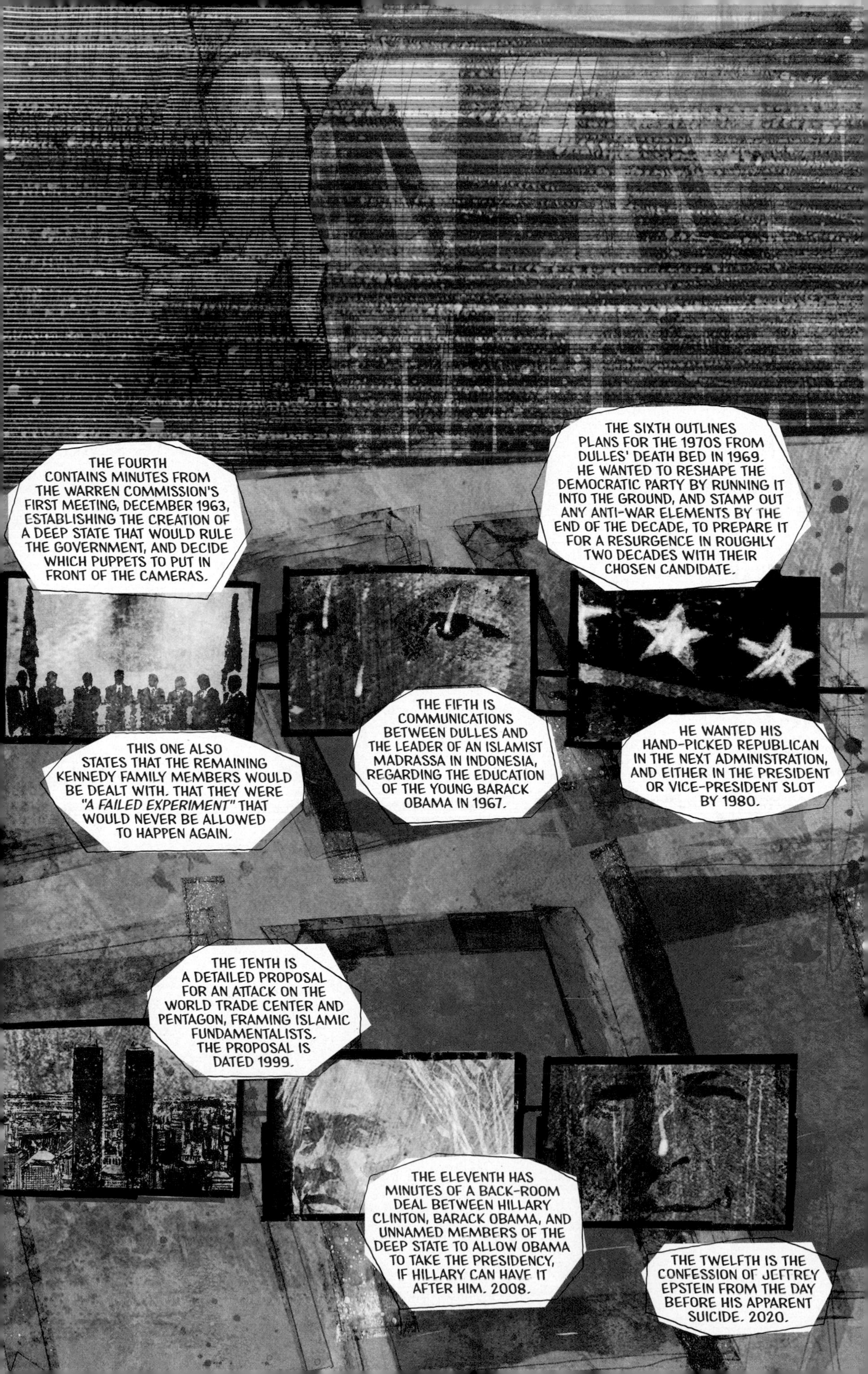
THE FOURTH CONTAINS MINUTES FROM THE WARREN COMMISSION'S FIRST MEETING, DECEMBER 1963, ESTABLISHING THE CREATION OF A DEEP STATE THAT WOULD RULE THE GOVERNMENT, AND DECIDE WHICH PUPPETS TO PUT IN FRONT OF THE CAMERAS.
THIS ONE ALSO STATES THAT THE REMAINING KENNEDY FAMILY MEMBERS WOULD BE DEALT WITH. THAT THEY WERE *"A FAILED EXPERIMENT"* THAT WOULD NEVER BE ALLOWED TO HAPPEN AGAIN.
THE FIFTH IS COMMUNICATIONS BETWEEN DULLES AND THE LEADER OF AN ISLAMIST MADRASSA IN INDONESIA, REGARDING THE EDUCATION OF THE YOUNG BARACK OBAMA IN 1967.
THE SIXTH OUTLINES PLANS FOR THE 1970S FROM DULLES' DEATH BED IN 1969. HE WANTED TO RESHAPE THE DEMOCRATIC PARTY BY RUNNING IT INTO THE GROUND, AND STAMP OUT ANY ANTI-WAR ELEMENTS BY THE END OF THE DECADE, TO PREPARE IT FOR A RESURGENCE IN ROUGHLY TWO DECADES WITH THEIR CHOSEN CANDIDATE.
HE WANTED HIS HAND-PICKED REPUBLICAN IN THE NEXT ADMINISTRATION, AND EITHER IN THE PRESIDENT OR VICE-PRESIDENT SLOT BY 1980.
THE TENTH IS A DETAILED PROPOSAL FOR AN ATTACK ON THE WORLD TRADE CENTER AND PENTAGON, FRAMING ISLAMIC FUNDAMENTALISTS. THE PROPOSAL IS DATED 1999.
THE ELEVENTH HAS MINUTES OF A BACK-ROOM DEAL BETWEEN HILLARY CLINTON, BARACK OBAMA, AND UNNAMED MEMBERS OF THE DEEP STATE TO ALLOW OBAMA TO TAKE THE PRESIDENCY, IF HILLARY CAN HAVE IT AFTER HIM. 2008.
THE TWELFTH IS THE CONFESSION OF JEFFREY EPSTEIN FROM THE DAY BEFORE HIS APPARENT SUICIDE. 2020.

SO...THOSE ARE THE PIECES, AND YOU AND I KNOW THEY AREN'T TRUE. BUT TELL ME THE FAIRY TALE. WEAVE IT ALL TOGETHER. PRETEND.
"ONCE UPON A TIME..."
SO, THE THEORY WOULD REST ON THE IDEA THAT PRESIDENTS AREN'T ELECTED, THEY ARE **CHOSEN.** AND WITH DULLES IN THE LEAD, THAT FINGERS THE MILITARY-INDUSTRIAL COMPLEX.
THE THEORY STARTS WITH THE MOTHER OF ALL CONSPIRACIES. THE MILITARY-INDUSTRIAL COMPLEX KILLED JFK FOR NOT BEING PLIABLE ENOUGH, AND THEN MADE SURE HIS SUCCESSORS **WOULD** BE.
THE CLINTONS AND THE BUSHES WERE PUPPETS OF THE DEEP STATE, PLACATED BY A SATANIC PEDOPHILE RING CONTROLLED BY JEFFREY EPSTEIN AND THE CIA.
THEY WERE PUSHED TO ENGINEER THE GLOBAL WAR ON TERRORISM BY STAGING 9/11, TO START THE FOREVER WARS IN THE MIDDLE EAST, AS A REPLACEMENT FOR THE COLD WAR.
ALL THE WHILE EXPANDING TRADE, COLONIZING THE ENTIRE PLANET WITH AMERICAN MONEY AND MILITARY MIGHT--AND KILLING ANYONE WHO GETS TOO CLOSE TO THE TRUTH OF THE NEW WORLD ORDER, AND ITS SECRET LEADERS.

OBAMA IS A KIND OF STRANGE ANTICHRIST FIGURE IN THIS MYTHOLOGY.
I MEAN, THE OBVIOUS IMPLICATION IS THAT DULLES WANTED OBAMA ELECTED PRESIDENT, THAT HE WAS PICKED FROM BIRTH TO ASSUME THE JOB, AND THEN RAISED AS A SECRET MUSLIM EXTREMIST...
MY GUESS, IF I READ THOSE DOCUMENTS, THEY'D SAY THAT OBAMA AND DULLES' GOAL WAS TO UNDERMINE AMERICAN VALUES AND REPLACE THEM WITH NEW GLOBALIST IDEALS TO HELP FURTHER AMERICAN MILITARY DOMINANCE OF THE ENTIRE PLANET.
ALL OF THIS CREATES A FEASIBLE BACKSTORY FOR THE STANDARD QANON CONSPIRACY. THE IDEA THAT PRESIDENT TRUMP WAS WAGING A SECRET WAR WITH A DEEP STATE HE SOUGHT TO EXPOSE BY LOCKING UP KEY PLAYERS IN THE DEMOCRATS' PEDOPHILE RINGS.

RIGHT. NOW THE TRICK IS NOT TO GET CAUGHT IN THE DETAILS. YOU START PULLING THREADS AND WE'LL GET NAZIS AND REPTILIANS AND THE ROTHSCHILDS PULLED INTO THIS MESS.
LOOK AT THE **BIG PICTURE.** WHAT **PURPOSE** DOES THIS STORY SERVE?
IT'S CREATING A UNIFIED HISTORY OF AMERICAN CONSPIRACY THEORIES, AND TYING THEM ALL TO THE MOST RECENT AND MOST DANGEROUS ONE.
TO WHAT END?
...
SEE, **THIS** IS THE WORK, KID. THIS IS HOW YOU NEED TO THINK. DON'T GET CAUGHT ON THE STORY ITSELF, THINK ABOUT HOW THE STORY IS BEING COLLECTED AND DELIVERED, AND FOR WHAT PURPOSE.
BLACK HAT DOESN'T GIVE A SHIT WHETHER JOE PUBLIC BELIEVES THAT THE CLINTONS WERE HAVING SEX WITH CHILDREN IN A PIZZA SHOP, OR THAT DUBYA BROUGHT DOWN THOSE TOWERS.
WHAT DOES IT **WANT** PEOPLE TO BELIEVE?
THAT THE GOVERNMENT HAS BEEN LYING ABOUT EVERYTHING FOR SIXTY YEARS. THAT OUR HISTORY IS ALL FICTION.
AND WHO **WROTE** THAT FICTION?
...
BLACK HAT IS TRYING TO EXPOSE THE EXISTENCE OF THE DEPARTMENT OF TRUTH.

I NEED YOU TO TELL ME RIGHT NOW THAT YOU DON'T BELIEVE ANY OF THIS, DAN.
22:000365686 >>
THERE WERE DAYS WHERE I GOT SWEPT UP IN IT...EACH OF THESE PIECES OF INFORMATION LEADS TO MORE RABBIT HOLES, AND IT'S SO EASY TO HEAD DOWN ONE AFTER ANOTHER.
22:000365686 >>
BUT THAT'S WHAT BOTHERED ME. ALL OF THESE MESSY STORIES FIT TOGETHER TOO NEATLY.
SOMEONE WAS TRYING TO PLAY ME. USE ME.
WHEN I REALIZED THAT, I STOPPED TRYING TO FIGURE OUT WHAT WAS INSIDE THOSE DOCUMENTS, AND I STARTED TRYING TO FIGURE OUT WHO WAS TRYING TO PLAY ME.
22:000365686 >>
22:000365686 >>
I DON'T UNDERSTAND.
THERE ARE ABOUT A HUNDRED CAMERAS AND MICROPHONES IN THIS ROOM. FROM EVERY ANGLE, WE'RE BEING WATCHED, AND PROBABLY RECORDED.
YOU REALIZE THAT SOUNDS AS CRAZY AS ANY ONE OF THOSE DOCUMENTS, DON'T YOU?
YEAH, I DO.
22:000365686 >>
22:000365686 >>

WHEN I TOLD YOU I HAD A STORY TO RUN, IT WASN'T THE ONES IN ALL THESE FOLDERS. IT'S THE ONE THAT ALL THESE FOLDERS IMPLY.
I'M JUST THE... I DON'T KNOW. I'M THE DELIVERY MECHANISM. THE BLANK PAGE THEY'RE USING TO SEND MESSAGES BACK AND FORTH.
THAT FIGHT IS THE STORY.
SO, WHAT DO YOU WANT TO DO?
22:0003656868

THIS... THIS IS THE STUFF WHERE I CAN'T TELL IF I'M NUTS OR NOT. BUT I THINK... THERE IS SOMEBODY TRYING TO PUT ALL OF THESE THEORIES IN THE WORLD.
AND THEN THERE'S SOMEBODY ELSE WATCHING ME, MAKING SURE I DON'T SPREAD A GODDAMN WORD.
SOMEONE IS TRYING TO WRITE A NEW HISTORY, AND SOMEONE ELSE IS TRYING TO STOP THEM FROM WRITING IT, AND I THINK IT'S BEEN HAPPENING FOR A LONG TIME.
BUT I KNOW THAT IF WE TRIED TO OUT THEM, THESE BITS OF EVIDENCE WOULD GET OUT INTO THE WILD, AND PEOPLE WOULD FIND THEM AND THEY'D GROW IN POWER.
AND THAT WOULD SELL A HELL OF A LOT OF NEWSPAPERS, AS WE WENT DOWN THE RABBIT HOLE, BUT EVEN BY REPORTING ALL OF IT AS FALSE, WE'D BE PUTTING IT IN THE WORLD, AND MAKING IT REAL.
I WANT TO TALK TO THEM. I WANT TO KNOW THE TRUTH SO I CAN GO TO SLEEP AT NIGHT, AND THEN I WANT TO PUT THIS ALL AWAY AND NEVER THINK ABOUT IT AGAIN.
HOW DO YOU PLAN ON DOING THAT?
WELL. WHOEVER IT IS, THEY'RE IN THE ROOM NEXT DOOR.

SHIT.
THIS ACTUALLY MAKES THINGS A BIT EASIER FOR US.
HOW DO YOU MEAN?
I WANTED YOU TO BE HERE TO HELP PUT THIS ONE TO BED. I NEED YOU TO START THINKING BIGGER, AND I NEED YOU TO PROVE THAT YOU HAVE THE BALLS TO DO WHAT NEEDS TO BE DONE.
WAIT...
YOU'RE GOING TO LET THEM INTO THE ROOM, AND THEN YOU'RE GOING TO SHOOT EACH OF THEM IN THE HEAD.
WHAT?!
SON, YOU KNOW HOW DANGEROUS THIS KNOWLEDGE CAN BE. IMAGINE TRYING TO DO OUR JOB WHEN THE GENERAL PUBLIC'S BELIEF IN THE ORGANIZATION STARTS SHAPING WHAT WE DO.
I'VE BEEN IN A SITUATION LIKE THAT BEFORE. IT GETS UGLY FAST. WE'RE MUCH, MUCH BETTER OFF NOT EXISTING.
22:000365686 >>

BUT HE SAID HE WANTS TO PUT IT TO SLEEP...
THE TRUTH DOESN'T GO TO SLEEP, COLE. HE LEARNS ABOUT OUR DEPARTMENT, AND HE'LL SEE US IN EVERY SHADOW IN WASHINGTON.
AND THEN ONE DAY HE GETS DRUNK IN A BAR, AND TELLS PEOPLE THAT WE TOOK HIS EVIDENCE OF A WHOLE SECRET HISTORY OF THE COUNTRY, AND THAT STARTS TO SPREAD ON ITS OWN.
AND EVERYTHING STARTS TO UNRAVEL AROUND US. BLACK HAT WINS, AND THEY GET THEIR FLAT EARTHS AND PEDOPHILE RINGS.
IS THAT WHAT YOU WANT, COLE?
JESUS.
YOU PROVE YOU CAN HANDLE THIS, AND I'LL LET YOU CHASE YOUR STAR-FACED MONSTER, AND ALL THE OTHER HORRIBLE THINGS YOU'LL FIND ALONG THE WAY.
22:0003656868 >>

KNOCK KNOCK
SHIT.
KIK
BUT IT'S UP TO YOU. I DON'T EXIST. IT'LL JUST BE YOU AND THEM IN THE ROOM.
HELLO?
UH...HI. THIS IS DANIEL CLAY. I'M A REPORTER FOR THE WASHINGTON POST. MY EDITOR AND I HAVE A FEW QUESTIONS FOR YOU.
YEAH... PLEASE COME IN.

IT'S NICE TO KNOW I WASN'T JUST BEING PARANOID.
I'M SURE.
WHAT ARE YOU? NSA? CIA?
NO. SOMETHING ELSE.
LOOK...AT THE END OF THE DAY, I AGREE WITH YOU GUYS. I DON'T WANT ANY OF THIS STORY TO RUN.
I DON'T EVEN WANT TO KNOW WHO YOU **ARE**...I JUST WANT TO KNOW...
YOU'RE THE GOOD GUYS, RIGHT?

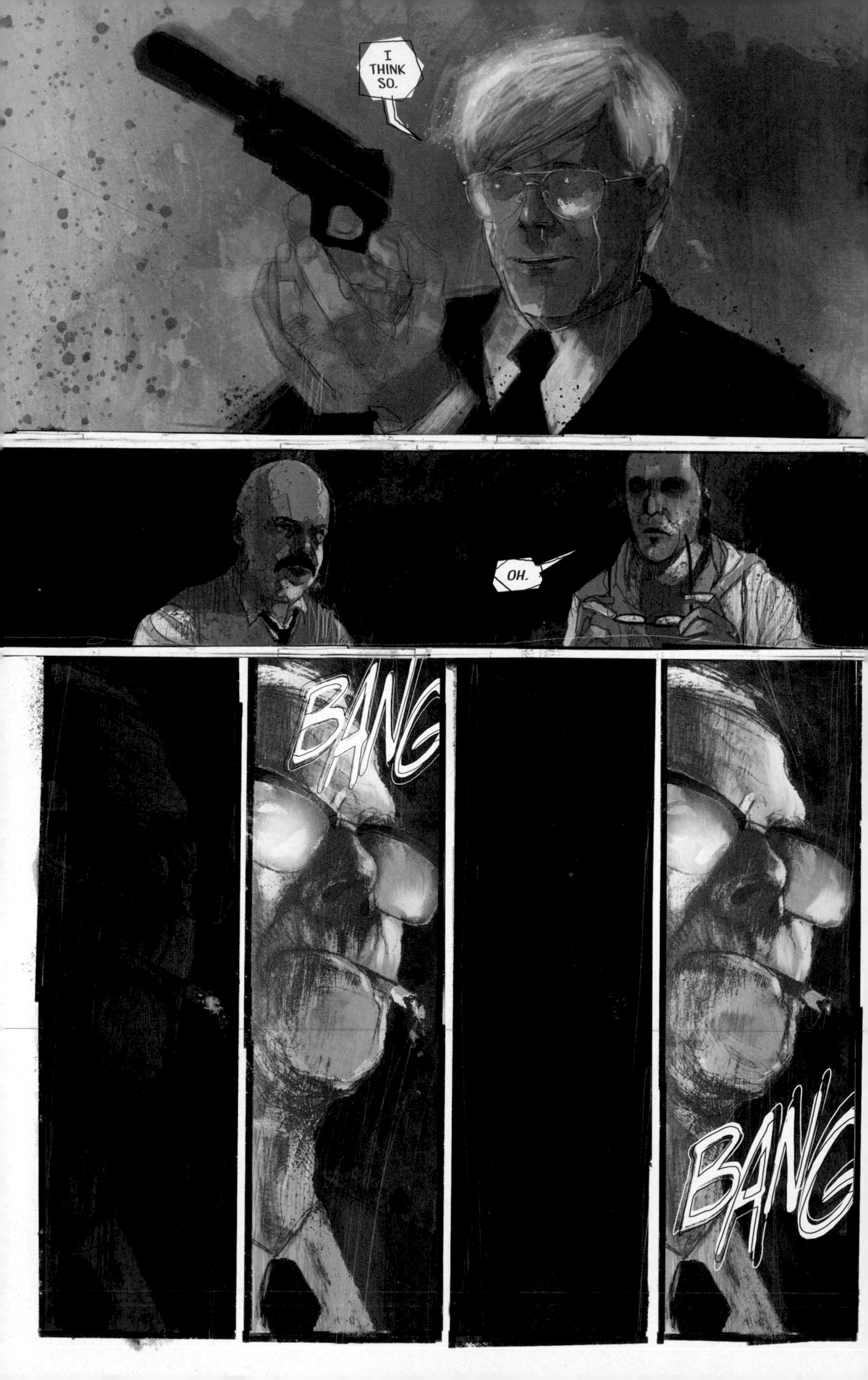
I THINK SO.
OH.
BANG
BANG

DEPARTMEN
UNITED STATE

CHAPTER 5 /

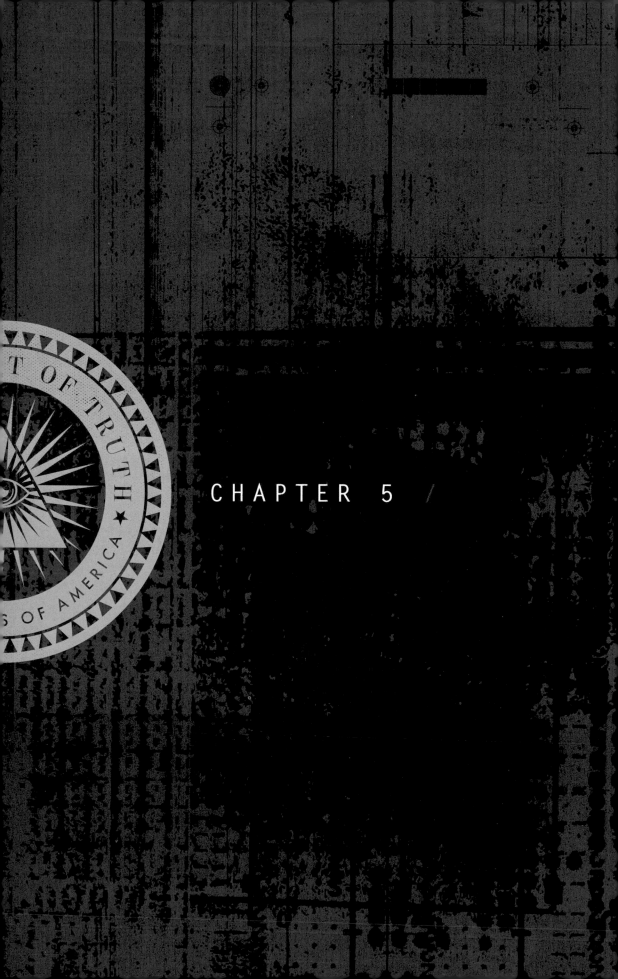

Action: failed
Status: 5.0.0
Diagnostic-Code: X-Postfix; Name service error
230
(1 of 3)
EPARTMENT OF DEFENSE
INVESTIGATION TASK FORCE (DEPLOYED)
GUANTANAMO BAY, CUBA
17 Dec 02
MO/J2
INTERROGATION SOP DTD 10 DEC 02
b(5)-1
"Decision Making" brief with the CG, you provided me a copy
GATION SOP dated 10 Dec 02 and asked me to review it and
However, I do want to reiterate CITF-G's general position on
emorandum for JTF GTMO dated 15 Nov 02, CITF-G
While the subject SOP clearly does not apply to
(applicable only to military and civilian interrogators assigned
ned for use in a battlefield environment as a means of
, to uncover enemy plans, determine enemy strength,
d logistical support, etc.)
investigating a wide variety of criminal and

DENVER INTERNATIONAL AIRPORT.

I'M IN.

OKAY, RUBY. THIS IS DOC. JUST GETTING UP TO SPEED... TELL ME WHAT YOU SEE.
WHERE'S COLE? HE'S SUPPOSED TO BE IN MY EAR.
THE DIRECTOR CALLED HIM IN.
HRM.
ARE YOU WEARING THE BLUETOOTH AGAIN?
YES, DOC.
YOU KNOW... YOU SHOULDN'T USE THOSE HEADPHONES. YOU SHOULD BE PROTECTING YOUR-SELF FROM ALL WIRELESS COMMUNICATION.
NOT REALLY POSSIBLE IN THIS DAY AND AGE...
CONSIDER YOUR ENEMIES, RUBY. THE ELECTRIC SIGNALS IN YOUR BRAIN CAN BE MANIPULATED...
YOU'RE READING TOO MANY OF YOUR OWN FILES. I'M GOING TO HAVE TO REPORT YOU TO LEE IF YOU KEEP SAYING THIS STUFF.
ALL YOU KIDS WONDER WHY THE WORLD WENT SIDEWAYS WHILE YOU'RE BEAMING THE ENTIRE INTERNET THROUGH YOUR BODY TWENTY-FOUR HOURS A DAY.

DOC.
THIS PLACE LOOKS EMPTY.
FALSE LEAD, THEN?
NO. I THINK THIS IS WHERE ALL THE DOSSIERS WERE MADE FOR BLACK HAT. BUT THEY SAW US COMING AND CLEARED OUT.
Don't worry. We made videosssss...

DON'T LISTEN TO HIM, RUBY. HE'S A FICTION... BLACK HAT LEFT HIM HERE TO TOY WITH YOU. THEY WANT YOU TO CLEAN UP THEIR LOOSE END.
Don't lisssten. We're underneath your cities...we hide in your human skin...
REPTILIAN.
NO, YOU AREN'T. AND NO, YOU DON'T.
YEAH.
THEY SHOULDN'T BE ABLE TO MANIFEST SO MANY OF THESE FUCKERS OUT OF SUCH A FRINGE THEORY. THEY SHOULDN'T BE ABLE TO DO ANY OF THIS.
SHIT.

WHAT IS IT?
IT'S NOT **EMPTY.** THERE'S BEEN A **MASSACRE** IN HERE.
I WANT TO...THANK YOU ALL FOR THE GOOD WORK YOU'VE DONE OVER THE LAST FEW MONTHS. YOU AND YOUR DEPARTMENT HAVE REALLY KEPT ME ON MY TOES.
BUT IT'S TOO LATE. WE'VE ALREADY DONE SO MUCH TO HELP TIP THE BALANCE AND DELIVER A NEW GREAT AWAKENING FOR THIS COUNTRY AND THE WORLD.
AND THEY LEFT A MESSAGE.
PRESS ENTER
THIS IS A DEAD END.
JESUS.
THAT BAD?
THEY PURGED THE FACILITY. KILLED THEIR OWN STAFF, **JUST** BECAUSE THEY KNEW WE WERE COMING.
AND THEY FILMED IT SO WE COULD **WATCH.**

HEHEHE HEHEHE.
AND TRUST US. WE KNOW DEAD.
THEY'RE TRYING TO CONTROL THEIR OWN DEFINITION. TEXTBOOK MOVE IN OUR FIELD...
THERE'S MORE.
WHAT'S GOING ON IN THERE?
YOU SAID THE DIRECTOR CALLED COLE IN?

CHAPTER FIVE The Shadow Play
I NEED TO TALK TO HIM. FAST.
COLE TURNER

YOU CAN GO HOME. WE HAVE PEOPLE WHO WILL CLEAN THIS UP.
OKAY.
TAKE A FEW DAYS.
OKAY.
WHEN YOU COME BACK, WE'LL TALK ABOUT YOUR STAR-FACED MAN.
YEAH.
YOU DID THE RIGHT THING, COLE.
SURE.

COLE?
HI.
WHAT'S WRONG?
MATTY... YOU KNOW I CAN'T TELL YOU.
OKAY, SHIT.
WHAT?
I WAS CALLING YOU BECAUSE THE OTHER COPY EDITORS DRAGGED ME OUT TO COLUMBIA HEIGHTS TO GET SHIT-FACED. IT'S SOMEBODY'S BIRTHDAY. I WAS GOING TO TRY TO GET YOU TO COME OUT, TOO.
SORRY. NOT TONIGHT.

WASHINGTON, DC.
CAR PARK
Matty
DO YOU WANT ME TO COME HOME?
NO. I THINK IT'LL BE GOOD IF I CAN CLEAR MY HEAD A BIT.
I SWEAR, I'LL TURN AROUND AND COME HOME RIGHT NOW.
PLEASE. YOU DON'T HAVE TO DO THAT.
OKAY. I LOVE YOU.
I LOVE YOU, TOO.

YOU'RE COLE TURNER.

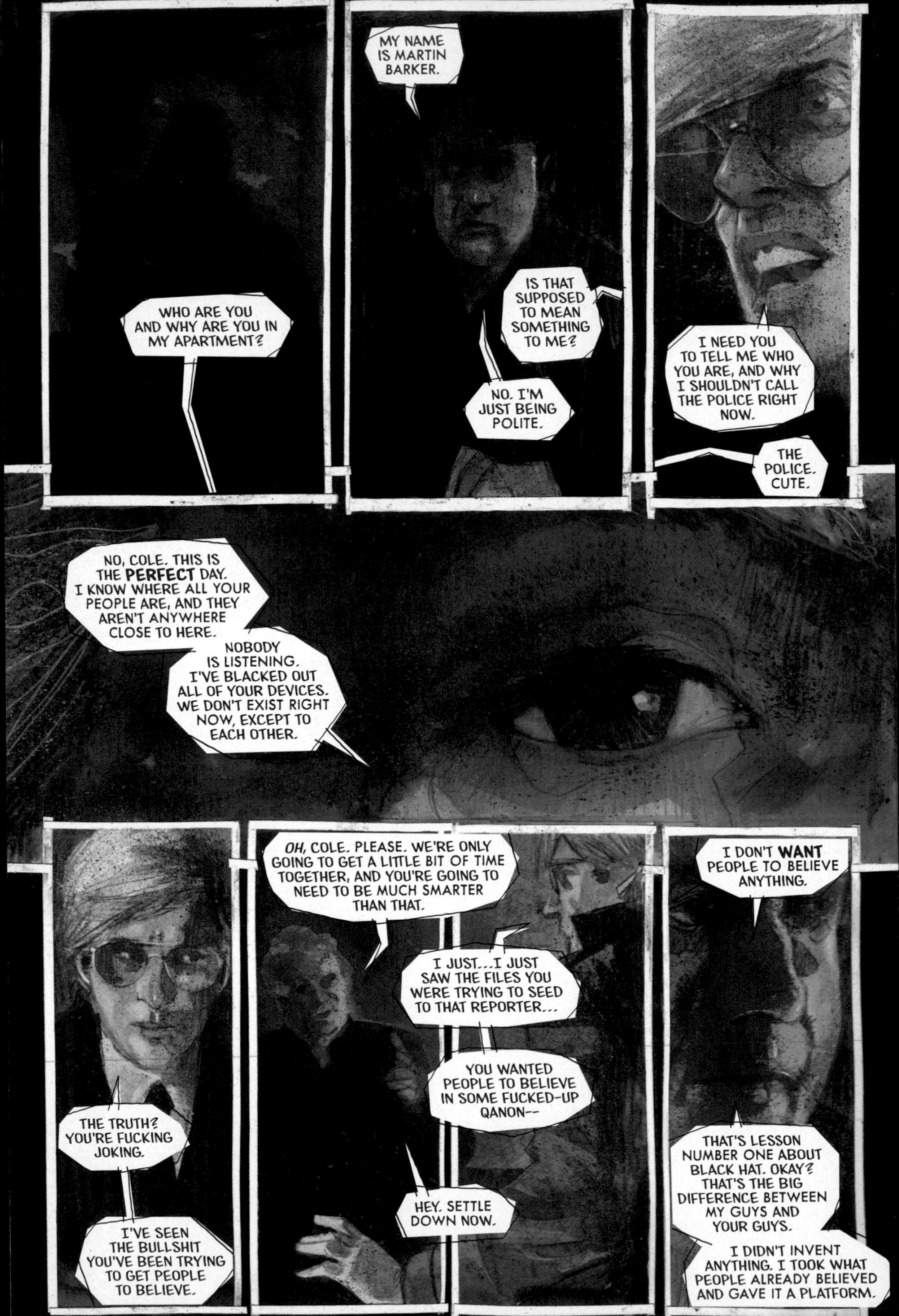
WHO ARE YOU AND WHY ARE YOU IN MY APARTMENT?
MY NAME IS MARTIN BARKER.
IS THAT SUPPOSED TO MEAN SOMETHING TO ME?
NO. I'M JUST BEING POLITE.
I NEED YOU TO TELL ME WHO YOU ARE, AND WHY I SHOULDN'T CALL THE POLICE RIGHT NOW.
THE POLICE. CUTE.
NO, COLE. THIS IS THE **PERFECT** DAY. I KNOW WHERE ALL YOUR PEOPLE ARE, AND THEY AREN'T ANYWHERE CLOSE TO HERE.
NOBODY IS LISTENING. I'VE BLACKED OUT ALL OF YOUR DEVICES. WE DON'T EXIST RIGHT NOW, EXCEPT TO EACH OTHER.
THE TRUTH? YOU'RE FUCKING JOKING.
I'VE SEEN THE BULLSHIT YOU'VE BEEN TRYING TO GET PEOPLE TO BELIEVE.
OH, COLE. PLEASE. WE'RE ONLY GOING TO GET A LITTLE BIT OF TIME TOGETHER, AND YOU'RE GOING TO NEED TO BE MUCH SMARTER THAN THAT.
I JUST...I JUST SAW THE FILES YOU WERE TRYING TO SEED TO THAT REPORTER...
YOU WANTED PEOPLE TO BELIEVE IN SOME FUCKED-UP QANON--
HEY. SETTLE DOWN NOW.
I DON'T **WANT** PEOPLE TO BELIEVE ANYTHING.
THAT'S LESSON NUMBER ONE ABOUT BLACK HAT. OKAY? THAT'S THE BIG DIFFERENCE BETWEEN MY GUYS AND YOUR GUYS.
I DIDN'T INVENT ANYTHING. I TOOK WHAT PEOPLE ALREADY BELIEVED AND GAVE IT A PLATFORM.

YOUR BOSS JUST CALLS ME *"THAT BLACK HAT FUCKER,"* WHICH WOULD HURT MY FEELINGS IF I DIDN'T KIND OF GET OFF ON IT. THAT ENOUGH FOR YOU TO PUT IT ALL TOGETHER?
YOU... RUN BLACK HAT.
BINGO. NOW, SIT DOWN. I WANT TO HAVE A CONVERSATION WITH YOU.
THERE IS **NOTHING** I WOULD HAVE TO SAY TO YOU ON MY BEST DAY, AND THIS IS **NOT** MY BEST DAY.
THAT MEANS I CAN SPEAK THE TRUTH.
SIX PERCENT OF AMERICANS BELIEVE THE MOON LANDING WAS FAKED. MORE THAN THAT BELIEVE THAT BARACK OBAMA WAS BORN IN KENYA.
WHY DON'T THEY HAVE THE RIGHT TO BELIEVE WHAT THEY WANT TO BELIEVE?
BECAUSE THOSE THINGS AREN'T TRUE.
BUT HERE'S THE THING, YOUNG PADAWAN. YOU'VE BEEN LET IN ON THE BIGGEST SECRET IN THE WORLD. YOU KNOW THAT WHEN IT COMES TO THE TRUTH, MAJORITY RULES.
WHY SHOULDN'T THE MAJORITY RULE, COLE?
BECAUSE... IT'S... IT'S IRRESPONSIBLE. PEOPLE GET HURT.

OH YEAH? HOW MANY PEOPLE HAVE I HURT SINCE YOU JOINED THE DEPARTMENT? BECAUSE BY MY MATH, YOUR SIDE HAS RACKED UP QUITE THE LITTLE BODY COUNT.
THEY EVEN GOT YOU IN ON IT, AND YOU'RE MADDER RIGHT NOW THAT YOU CAN'T GO CRYING INTO YOUR PILLOW THAN YOU ARE THAT I'M SITTING HERE.
NO, I'M PRETTY MAD YOU'RE SITTING THERE.
OKAY, SO YOUR DEPARTMENT IS IN THE MORAL RIGHT, THEN. MY BAD. I DIDN'T UNDERSTAND.
WE SHOULD JUST KILL EVERYONE WHO DOESN'T BELIEVE THE RIGHT THINGS? IT'S A NICE IDEA. IT EVEN WORKS FOR A BIT.
YOU SHOULD ASK SOME OF THE OLD FOGIES ON YOUR SIDE ABOUT THEIR SOVIET COUNTERPART BACK IN THE DAY.
WHAT THE 20TH CENTURY WOULD LOOK LIKE NOW, IF THE BERLIN WALL CAME DOWN THE OTHER WAY AROUND. BOY, I'M TELLING YOU.
LOOK, COLE. I'M A STUDENT OF HISTORY. I HAVE TO BE, IN THIS LUNATIC WORLD, BUT I'M GOING DOWN A RABBIT HOLE.
I JUST CAME HERE TO MAKE YOU UNDERSTAND A FEW TRUE THINGS.

THE FIRST TRUTH...
THIS GAME WE'RE PLAYING. IT'S BEEN GOING ON FOR A LONG FUCKING TIME. THAT'S THE ONE **REAL** CONSPIRACY OUT THERE. THE ACTUAL SECRET HISTORY OF OUR WORLD.
IHS
G
THERE HAVE BEEN PLAYERS IN EVERY GREAT CIVILIZATION WHO HAVE KNOWN THE TRUE NATURE OF REALITY, AND WHO HAVE TRIED TO PLAY THE PEOPLE TO EMPOWER THEMSELVES.
YOUR SIDE HAS THE HARD COPY HISTORIES. THEY STOLE THEM OUT OF EUROPE IN WW2 AND USED THEM TO CREATE THE DEPARTMENT OF TRUTH.

THE SECOND TRUTH...
THE DEPARTMENT OF TRUTH WAS **NOT** FORMED TO UPHOLD OUR BETTER FUCKING ANGELS OR ANY STUPID GODDAMN THING LIKE THAT.
IT WAS FORMED TO RESHAPE THE POSTWAR WORLD WITH AMERICA AT ITS CENTER, RATHER THAN ALL THE IMPERIAL POWERS OF THE PREVIOUS TWO HUNDRED YEARS.
THE PEOPLE WHO CONTROL THE TRUTH CONTROL THE WORLD. I BELIEVE THE AMERICANS WHO BUILT YOUR DEPARTMENT DID IT WITH A GOOD DREAM IN THEIR HEARTS. AN ADMIRABLE DREAM, IF NOT A REALISTIC ONE.
BUT HERE'S THE THIRD TRUTH, COLE...
THAT WHOLE FUCKING DREAM STARTED TO FALL APART ON NOVEMBER 22ND, 1963.

WHY ARE YOU TELLING ME ANY OF THIS?
YOU'RE ON THE WRONG SIDE OF THIS FIGHT, KID.
YOU ARE WORKING WITH THE BAD GUYS, TRYING TO KEEP A STRANGLEHOLD ON THE TRUTH IN THE NAME OF A DREAM THAT DIED SIXTY YEARS AGO.
AND I KNOW YOU FEEL IT. YOU JUST SHOT AND KILLED TWO PEOPLE, COLE, AND I CAN SEE YOU'RE STILL IN SHOCK. THAT'S SENSIBLE.
THAT'S JUST FUCKING HUMAN.
YOU KNOW, THAT NICE HUSBAND OF YOURS. HE'S OUT WITH HIS WORK FRIENDS RIGHT NOW.
HE MIGHT EVEN BE OUT LATE ENOUGH TO GET THE NEWS THAT AN EDITOR AND A WRITER FROM HIS PAPER JUST GOT ASSASSINATED.
YOU REALIZE YOU'RE GOING TO BE INVITED TO THE FUNERAL, RIGHT? DO YOU THINK YOU HAVE IT IN YOU TO KEEP LYING TO HIM--FIND THE RIGHT EXCUSES TO SKIP THE SERVICE?
YOU CAN'T BUILD THINGS ON A LIE.
NOW, YOU DON'T REALLY BELIEVE ANY OF THIS, AND THAT'S OKAY. IT'S GOING TO TAKE SOME TIME, BUT I'M GOING TO HELP YOU CONNECT A DOT REAL QUICK.

FLASHBACK TO THE LATE '70s, EARLY '80s. THE REAL START OF YOUR BOSS LEE'S REIGN OVER THE DEPARTMENT OF TRUTH. THE COUNTRY'S GETTING ALL NOSTALGIC FOR THAT KIND OF FULL-ON, 1950s-STYLE POSTWAR AMERICANA.
AND THE DEPARTMENT IS GETTING NOSTALGIC IN ITS OWN WAY FOR THE POWER IT USED TO WIELD OVER THE AMERICAN DREAM. ONLY TROUBLE IS THEY WEEDED OUT ALL THE COMMIES A FEW DECADES EARLIER.
BUT LEE KNOWS THAT REAGAN'S NOT GOING TO GET HIS SHINING CITY ON THE HILL WITHOUT SOME DEVILS HIDING IN THE SHADOWS.
YOU'RE LYING.
I HAVEN'T SAID ONE LIE TO YOU YET, AND YOU KNOW IT.
THE SATANIC PANIC WAS JUST THE NEWER, WEIRDER TAKE ON THE OLD RED SCARE, BUT THIS TIME THE RED CAME WITH POINTY HORNS AND A PITCHFORK.
I'M NOT SAYING THEY COOKED IT UP, BUT THEY HELPED IT SPREAD...
FROM A COUPLE OF PAPERBACK BOOKS TO SOME PRESCHOOLS, ALL THE WAY TO LITTLE COLE TURNER IN WISCONSIN, AND HIS WONDERFUL IMAGINATION.
AND WHAT CAME OUT OF IT.

HIIIIIII, COLE...
OH, I'M HUNNNNNGRY.
I JUSSST CAME FROM A PIZZA PARTY, BUT I'M STILL HUNNNNGRY. HEHEHEHEHE.
NO!
I WAS SO FUCKING MAD WHEN THEY PULLED YOU OUT OF MY GRASP. WE HAD YOU ON THE PLANE AND EVERYTHING. WE SHOWED YOU THE END OF THE WORLD.
BUT I HAD YOU PEGGED WRONG. I THOUGHT YOU WERE MORE OF A TRUE BELIEVER TYPE. YOU WANTED PROOF, SO I GAVE YOU PROOF.
BUT THAT'S NOT WHAT YOU WERE CHASING AFTER ALL, WAS IT? IT'S ALWAYS BEEN HIM. AND FUCK, HE'S BEEN A USEFUL ASSET FOR THE TEAM. YOU'LL SEE WHEN YOU COME OVER TO OUR SIDE.

I'D NEVER...
YOOUUU'RE A MEAN LITTLE BOY.
ALWAYS BEEN SOOOO MEAN.
I'VE ALREADY KILLED TWO PEOPLE TONIGHT.
AND IT'S FUCKING KILLING YOU.
LOOK. I REALIZE I'M NOT GOING TO CONVINCE YOU RIGHT AWAY. YOU NEED TO GET THERE ON YOUR OWN. I RESPECT THAT.
BUT YOU'VE GOT A BIGGER ROLE TO PLAY THAN YOU REALIZE. SHE'S GOT HER EYES ON YOU. SHE'S BEEN WATCHING FOR A LONG, LONG TIME.
THE WOMAN IN RED...WHO IS SHE...WHAT IS SHE?
THAT'S THE MILLION-DOLLAR QUESTION, ISN'T IT?
GET INTO THOSE ARCHIVES, COLE. THERE'S STILL SO MUCH YOU NEED TO LEARN ABOUT HOW THIS WORLD WORKS.
JUST REMEMBER. THEY PUT THIS DEMON IN YOUR HEAD TO TRY AND CONTROL YOU. I TOOK IT OUT OF YOUR HEAD TO FREE EVERY-BODY.
I'LL BE IN TOUCH, KIDDO.
SEEEE YOUUUU SOON.

WHERE IS HE?
HE...HE WENT IN THERE...
IS THERE ANOTHER WAY OUT OF THE APARTMENT?
NO.
WELL, HE FOUND ONE.
RUBY...WHY DID YOU AND LEE PICK ME? WHY DIDN'T YOU KILL ME AT THE END OF THE WORLD?
I THOUGHT I KNEW.

BLACK HAT...THEY'VE BEEN WATCHING YOU YOUR ENTIRE LIFE. THEY ARRANGED FOR YOU TO BE AT THAT CONFERENCE. THEY WERE TRYING TO RECRUIT YOU.
I THINK LEE KNEW THAT. I THINK HE WANTED TO BEAT THEM TO IT.
BUT WHY?! WHY ME?!
I DON'T KNOW, COLE, I REALLY DON'T KNOW.

DEPARTMENT OF TRUTH

UNITED STATES OF AMERICA

ALSO AVAILABLE FROM TINY ONION
FIND OUT MORE AT READRAZORBLADES.COM
RAZORBLADES © 2021 JAMES TYNION IV & STEVE FOXE. BIRD EATER © 2021 JEN BARTEL.